I0819481

Whitney navy revolver

(Courtesy The Whitney Library, The New Haven Museum)

The Whitney Navy Revolver
A Reference of the Models and Types 1857-1866

Daniel E. Williams, Jr.

Schiffer Military History
Atglen, PA

Dedication

This book is dedicated to Stacey, Marc, and Terri for their support and encouragement with this project, and to the collectors and historians who share my interest in the Whitney Navy Revolver.

Book Design by Ian Robertson.

Copyright © 2012 by Daniel E. Williams, Jr.
Library of Congress Control Number: 2012945064

All rights reserved. No part of this work may be reproduced or used in any form or by any means—graphic, electronic, or mechanical, including photocopying or information storage and retrieval systems—without written permission from the publisher.

The scanning, uploading and distribution of this book or any part thereof via the Internet or via any other means without the permission of the publisher is illegal and punishable by law. Please purchase only authorized editions and do not participate in or encourage the electronic piracy of copyrighted materials.

"Schiffer," "Schiffer Publishing, Ltd. & Design," and the "Design of pen and inkwell" are registered trademarks of Schiffer Publishing, Ltd.

Printed in China.
ISBN: 978-0-7643-4249-3

We are interested in hearing from authors with book ideas on related topics.

Published by Schiffer Publishing, Ltd.
4880 Lower Valley Road
Atglen, PA 19310
Phone: (610) 593-1777
FAX: (610) 593-2002
E-mail: Info@schifferbooks.com.
Visit our web site at: www.schifferbooks.com
Please write for a free catalog.
This book may be purchased from the publisher.
Try your bookstore first.

In Europe, Schiffer books are distributed by:
Bushwood Books
6 Marksbury Avenue
Kew Gardens
Surrey TW9 4JF, England
Phone: 44 (0) 20 8392-8585
FAX: 44 (0) 20 8392-9876
E-mail: Info@bushwoodbooks.co.uk.
Visit our website at: www.bushwoodbooks.co.uk
Try your bookstore first.

CONTENTS

Epigraph

Whitney's Revolvers are equal to any in market. They are made of the best materials, and in a superior manner. Besides being better balanced, they are more accurate shooters than the old style Repeating Pistols, most in use, because the barrel is more firmly held to the cylinder, so that there is no yielding, or springing apart, when the ball leaves the cylinder to slug through the barrel.

Eli Whitney, Jr. (in his price list to the Ordnance Department, January 1860)

ACKNOWLEDGMENTS

There are many people and many sources that contributed data for this study. Data was gathered using written survey information and e-mail correspondence and images, as well as online photographs. The author wishes to acknowledge the following sources with a special thank you:

William Lee, a fellow collector whose interest and observations regarding the Whitney Navy revolver helped provide guidance for the author's research.

Marc Williams, who developed and updated the online survey website and assisted in locating Whitney revolvers for the database.

Stacey Oxendine and Stefanie Williams for proofreading the manuscript.

Jim Slayton, for his assistance in providing unpublished research from the late Ken Domina and the late Don Ware.

The late Ken Domina and the late Don Ware for information compiled in the mid-1990s. This data included correspondence between E. Whitney and the Bureau of Ordnance in the 1850s and during the Civil War, as well as other data compiled on martial Whitney revolvers.

Heather Dawn Beattie, Museum Collections Manager, Virginia Historical Society. A special thank you is extended to VHS and to Ms. Beattie for allowing the author to examine the Whitney revolver of General J.E.B. Stuart, and to publish a photograph of that revolver in this book.

Hayes Otoupalik for providing photographs and survey data for several rare revolvers, including First Model Whitney revolvers, First and Second Model Spiller & Burr revolvers, and a T.W. Cofer revolver.

Norm Flayderman, for the existing data he has provided and for his encouragement to the author to complete this study.

Brent Wiburn, Antique Arms Inc., for the use of several of his excellent photographs on our website, and for linking the Whitney survey site to his website.

The following Auction Companies for providing photographs of special interest and rare revolvers:

Cowan's Auctions Inc., Cincinnati, OH
www.cowanauctions.com

James D. Julia Auctioneers, Fairfield, ME
www.jamesdjulia.com

Greg Martin Auctions, San Francisco, CA
www.gregmartinauctions.com

Rock Island Auction Company, Moline, IL
www.rockislandauction.com

Many other individuals and businesses contributed data on Whitney revolvers, photographs, or other information that made this book possible. The author is grateful to each of these contributors:

R.J. Askeland
Austin History Center, Austin Public Library
John Bielamowicz
Paul Bowman
Stephen Burgess, Campsite Artifacts
Ed Bushardt
Cliff Carlisle
Christer Cederroth
John Clark
Marvin Cook
Calvin Coolidge
Gary Creager
Tad Davidson
Dan Donaghy
Anthony Daum
Brian Dunn
David Edwards
Darrel Favrhow
Matthew Fleming, The Civil War Image Shop
John Fox
Paul Fraser
Edward Gagnon
Denis Gaubert
Bob Glennon
John Glosser
Hugh Goldsmith
Frank Graves
Greensboro Historical Museum, Greensboro, NC
Petro Groendijk
Cade Gunnells
James Hambright
Patrick Hancock
William Heavenor
Emery Henderson
John C. Hill
Michael Hoffman
Peter B. Hollis
Paul Houghton
Michael Humphrey and Delpha Weatherson
William Hurlock
Charles Isgrig
Todd James
Lyle Jorgensen
Jason Kaplan, J&J Military Antiques
Neil Kenney
Lorne Kloepfer
Ed Kushner
Bruce Kusrow
David Lienhart
Terry Ludlow
Richard MacDonald
Grant McLean
Colin Mahle
Merz Antique Firearms
Greg Mills
NC State Historic Sites & Properties
Mike Norman
NRA Firearms Museum
Anders Olsson
Stephen Osman
Lawrence Parker
Charles Pate
Tony W. Penland
Powerhouse Museum, Sydney, Australia
Tim Prince, College Hill Arsenal
Frank Privett
Jeff Reading
James A. Rogers
Peter Schiffers
Randall Setty
Ron Shaiman
Mark Smith
Tom Smith
Brian Springer
John Tetley
Jack Thomas, Sr.
Johan Tiffin
George Tondryk
William Upton
Claude Vallet
Thomas "Rusty" VanLandingham
Luis Castillo Vargas
VMI Museum, Lexington VA.
Vladimir - Slovakia
WilliamWebb
Hans Westberg
West Point Museum Collections
Eli Whitney Museum
The Whitney Library, The New Haven Museum
William Willis
Wilson's Creek National Battlefield, National Park Service
Dave Ziska
Mike Zorn

Eli Whitney, Jr., 1820 - 1894. (*Photo courtesy of Cowan's Auctions Inc.*)

INTRODUCTION

The Whitney Navy Revolver has often been seen as just another Civil War revolver that perhaps pales in comparison to the Colt Revolvers of that era. However, Whitney Revolvers have a story of their own to tell. In fact, if not for the Whitney Firearms facility that manufactured Colt's Whitneyville Walker Revolver, Samuel Colt's business may not have achieved the later success and fame that it did. More of the history of Whitney Firearms will be discussed in Chapter One.

Whitney Revolvers were in use prior to the Civil War, and many were purchased for use during the war. These revolvers were perhaps the first "solid frame" pistols to go into production, and they soon evolved into very sturdy weapons with several improvements over other revolvers of their day. Due to its reliability and solid construction, the Whitney revolver saw use not only in the armies of the North and South, but on the Western Frontier as well.

The focus of this book is Whitney's "Navy" Revolver, which would become his most well known and widely used revolver. The term "Navy" revolver refers to the medium frame size of this revolver and the 36 caliber ball it used, rather than to its use by the Navy. In fact, only about 18% of these revolvers were sold to the U.S. Navy.

The purpose of this book is to assist collectors to better identify the various models and types of the Whitney Navy Revolver, and to provide some insight into the development and use of this firearm. While the centerpiece of this book is the updated classification of the models and types of the Whitney Navy Revolver, there is much more that the author found necessary to include: the history behind the development of this classic revolver; the use of this revolver by both North and South during the Civil War; the engraved examples; the cartridge conversions; and the use of Whitney revolvers in England and Australia were all areas of interest that needed to be included.

This book was inspired in part by a friend of the author, and fellow collector, William Lee. We both shared a common interest in the Whitney Navy Revolver, and as our interest grew, each of us obtained examples of these revolvers. We then endeavored to learn as much as we could, but quickly determined that there was very little in writing regarding these firearms. Most of the available information had been written 40 or more years ago. Much of our research was conducted by reviewing the various examples we could find, both in person and online. The author then decided to conduct a survey, which he hoped would be beneficial in further analyzing the models and the various types of this revolver. A survey form was designed and made available online in order to increase the availability of the survey to as many people as possible. Marc Williams, the author's son, developed the website, which contained an introduction to the research project, survey forms, and reference material. His technical assistance, along with his interest in the Whitney Navy revolver, is most appreciated. The website was designed to be used during the survey period of approximately two and a half years.

As more was learned about these fine revolvers, it was decided to compile these findings into a book for the benefit of other collectors and firearms enthusiasts. While this book may serve as a reference work for the Whitney Navy Revolver, it is also a tribute to Eli Whitney, Jr. and the improvements he made to the revolvers of his time.

Before proceeding with this book, the author contacted Mr. Norm Flayderman, whose *Guide to Antique American Firearms* the author has long used as a primary reference. The information found in Mr. Flayderman's *Guide* has been invaluable to collectors in identifying the changing features of the Whitney revolver as improvements were made during its manufacture. In regard to this study, Mr. Flayderman indicated he was pleased to learn of the Whitney research project and encouraged the author to follow it through to completion. He further stated that "***the field is really begging for a good up-to-date study and reference...***" Mr. Flayderman further stated that it has been over 35 years since an unpublished manuscript by Mr. Charles Thrower was used to glean data on Whitney revolvers. The number of revolvers surveyed for that manuscript, or methods used, have been lost to time. *The Whitney Navy Revolver* is the result of a survey of 370 Whitney Navy Revolvers and the findings related to those revolvers.

This book is in no way meant to discredit any prior studies. All available information that could be located was used as a basis for this study.

While this book will reference some of the existing knowledge of the "Models and Types" of the Whitney Navy Revolver, the author will use the findings of his survey to refine these characteristics and redefine the corresponding serial number ranges. The additional chapters on martial revolvers; Whitneys for the South; the influence of Whitney revolvers on Confederate revolvers; the conversion to cartridge guns; and examples of engraved revolvers should be of interest to all readers. Regardless of whether you are a collector or just have an interest in historical firearms, it is the author's hope that you will find this book useful as a reference. This research has by no means uncovered all there is to know about Eli Whitney and his Navy Revolver, but perhaps it has shed some new light on a very important American firearm. This book may also serve as a fresh starting point for even further research.

Survey Methods and Results

This research project began with a survey form that could be accessed online at www.whitneyrevolver.com. This survey could be completed and returned by e-mail or printed and returned by mail. A copy of the survey form is found in Appendix D. For anyone without computer access, a survey form could also be requested by mail.

The Internet has been very valuable in conducting this research. Many revolvers could be found online with the serial numbers posted and photographs provided. In those cases where photographs were adequate for examining the revolver, and where sufficient information could be obtained from the owner, that data was included in the survey. The use of an Internet website allowed this research project to reach beyond the borders of the United States, obtaining survey data on revolvers as far away as Australia, Peru, Chile, the Netherlands, Sweden, Slovakia, France, Canada, England, and Scotland.

Data was obtained for 370 Whitney Navy Revolvers. The following tables provide the number and percentage of surveys obtained for each Model and Type.

For comparison, the first two columns will provide the number and percentage of revolver production by Model and Type.

First Model

Data for the First Model Whitney Navy Revolver was found to be very scarce. It has been estimated that only 1,500 of the First Model revolvers were produced. This survey yielded too few revolvers to validate any existing data. The earliest serial numbers located were numbers 2 and 23. Other serial numbers were found in the 100, 600, and 900 ranges. Two revolvers in the 900 serial number range prompted the author to adjust the approximate serial number ranges for the 3rd and 4th types. According to existing research, along with the author's limited findings, the types of First Model revolvers fall into the serial number ranges shown below:

Type	Serial Number Range	Number Produced	Percent Produced
1st	1-100	100	6.7%
2nd	100-300	200	13.3%
3rd	300-1000	700	46.7%
4th	1000-1500	500	33.3%
Total		1500	100.0%

Second Model

The following table is the author's analysis of the Second Model Navy Revolver.

The Second Model serial numbers began again with the number 1 and went to approximately 34000. The highest number found in the author's database was 32862; however, serial number 33879 was reported in a letter by the late Mr. Ken Domina as being in his personal collection.

Type	Serial Number Range	Number Produced	Percent Produced	Revolvers Surveyed	Percent of Surveys
1st	1-2000	2000	5.9%	28	7.7%
2nd	2000-6000	4000	11.8%	67	18.5%
3rd	6000-11000	5000	14.7%	41	11.3%
4th	11000-28000	17000	50.0%	192	52.9%
5th	28000-34000	6000	17.6%	35	9.6%
Total		34000	100.0%	363	

The largest number of revolvers surveyed were of the Second Model, 4th Type. This was no surprise, since the largest number of revolvers produced were of that Type. There were approximately 17,000 of the 4th Type produced, and the majority of the martially marked revolvers were found in this "Type."

All respondents to this survey, as well as many other contributors, are listed in the acknowledgments section of this book. The contributions of everyone who made this study possible are greatly appreciated.

Results

The analysis of this study yielded some interesting information regarding Whitney revolvers, and provided some insight into possible years of production. These findings also led the author to include chapters on martially marked Whitney revolvers, as well as those used in the Confederacy.

Most importantly, there was an obvious need to redefine some of the serial number ranges as the characteristics of the revolvers changed. The characteristics of each "Model" and "Type", along with serial number ranges, will be found in Chapter Four. Photographs are also included for every "Type" of the two "Models" of the Whitney Navy revolver.

Finally, the author obtained an even greater appreciation for the Whitney Navy Revolver and its inventor, as well as for its service during and after the "War Between the States."

It is hoped the reader will share, or gain, this same appreciation.

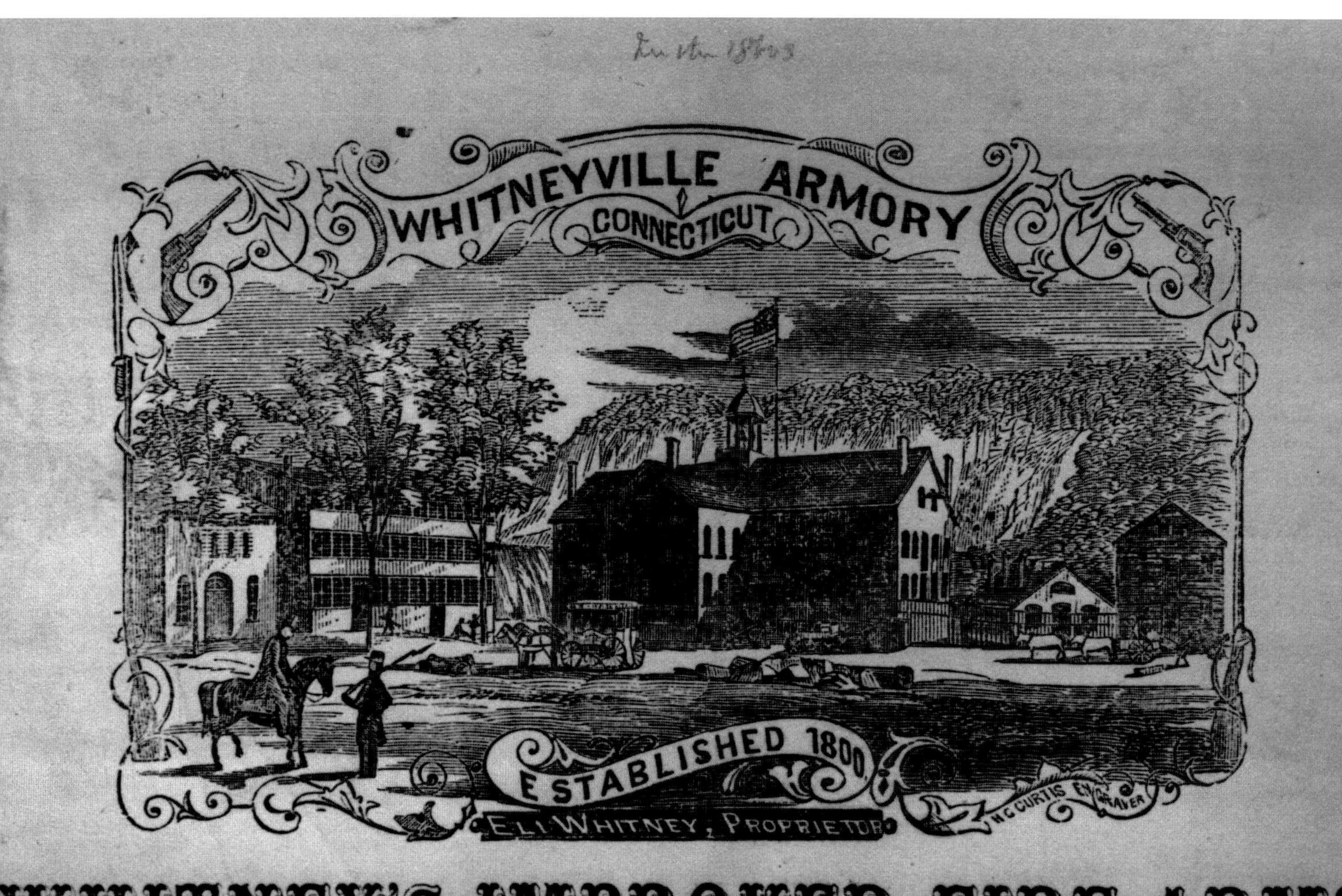

(Courtesy The Whitney Library, The New Haven Museum)

1

A BRIEF HISTORY OF WHITNEY FIREARMS

Many people remember learning in school of Eli Whitney and his invention of the cotton gin. However, few people realize what followed in his effort to market his invention and how he became involved in the manufacture of firearms. Whitney constructed his first model of the cotton gin in late 1792; however, his invention did not receive a patent until 1794. In the meanwhile, there were infringements on his patent and other copies of his cotton gin were produced. He failed in the courts to resolve this situation and many imitations of his cotton gin reached the market. Therefore, Whitney lost the opportunity to dominate the cotton gin industry, and to profit from his invention.[1]

In 1798, he turned his interest and energies to the manufacture of muskets for the United States Army. He purchased land in what is now Whitneyville, within a few miles of New Haven, Connecticut. When he began this venture he had no workers, no capital, and knew nothing about making muskets. Even though he had no experience, he was able to obtain a contract from the United States government based on his reputation as an inventor. Whitney's greatest contribution, and subsequent success in gaining Government contracts, stemmed from his manufacturing process and use of "interchangeable parts." The use of interchangeable parts helped eliminate the problems associated with unique, one-of-a-kind weapons. If one part, or mechanism, in a weapon failed, a new piece could be installed and the weapon would not have to be discarded.[2]

Despite heavy expenses, Whitney was able to fulfill this first contract. Other government contracts were to follow, and Whitney Firearms Company became prosperous prior to Eli Whitney's death in 1825 at the age of 59. Whitney's only son was Eli Whitney, Jr. born five years prior to Whitney's death. Since his son was a minor, the firearms business was temporarily managed by Philos and Eli Whitney Blake, the nephews of Whitney. Whitney had taken these nephews into the business sometime following his contract of July 18, 1812, with the U.S. Government for 15,000 muskets. The Blakes operated the armory until 1834, at which time James Goodrich and Henry Edwards, interim trustees of Whitney's estate, operated the facility.[3]

After attending school at Yale and Princeton, Eli Whitney, Jr. returned to New Haven to assume control of his father's armory in 1841. Eli Whitney, Jr. successfully operated the Whitney Arms Company until it was sold to the Winchester Repeating Arms Company in 1888. During this period Whitney not only expanded the Armory, but also constructed New Haven's first waterworks on the site. He began that project in 1860, and by January 1862 water had begun to flow through the company's pipes and into homes and hydrants throughout the city. Whitney was well known for his public service and generosity to his community.[4]

When Eli Whitney, Jr. took control of the Whitney Arms Company in 1841, the armory was actively involved in the production of muskets. Contracts for muskets would continue to be a mainstay for Whitney throughout the Civil War. In the early 1850s Whitney began producing his first revolvers. These first handguns were not what we would recognize as a revolver today, due to the patent that Samuel Colt held on the revolving mechanism. In order to avoid infringing on Colt's patent, Whitney used a variety of techniques to turn the cylinder, such as turning it by hand, and later the use of a separate trigger to rotate the cylinder.

Of those percussion revolvers that were invented during the early 19th century, the Colt revolvers were certainly the most famous and widely used. Almost everyone knows Sam Colt was a clever businessman as well as an inventor; but many people do not realize that Eli Whitney, Jr. was a contemporary of Sam Colt, and would also become a manufacturer of fine revolvers. Whitney was also to have the unique position of helping Colt salvage and develop his business, and later to compete with Colt in the sale of revolvers.

The first successful Colt revolver was the Paterson model, which was produced from 1836 to 1842. Problems with military contracts, the economic crash of 1837, and loss of payments for Paterson pistols sent to Florida during the Seminole War resulted in the closure of the Colt plant in Paterson, New Jersey, in late 1843. Then, Sam Colt received a government contract for 1,000 revolvers after the start of the Mexican War. Colt re-entered the firearms business in 1847 with the "Walker" Colt. This was the largest and most powerful black powder repeating handgun ever made, and it was manufactured at the firearms plant of Eli Whitney, Jr. Since Sam Colt did not have a firearms manufacturing facility when the opportunity came to produce the Walker Colt, he contracted with Whitney Firearms Company for 1,100 of these revolvers, later known as the Whitneyville Walkers. Thus, Colt reestablished and positioned himself in the emerging firearms market, and Whitney had prepared his own company for the future manufacture of revolvers.

Whitney, as well as other arms manufacturers, found themselves at a disadvantage as they entered the revolver market. Sam Colt held the patent on his revolving mechanism, which meant that Whitney would need to completely redesign the method of revolving the cylinder on his handguns. It was not until 1850 that Whitney produced his first "revolver." The Whitney Hooded Cylinder Pocket Revolver held six rounds in a hooded cylinder. A button on the top rear of the frame was used to release the cylinder so it could be revolved by hand. Approximately 200 of these 28 caliber firearms were produced.

Around 1852 Whitney developed his Two Trigger Pocket Revolver. One trigger, located forward of the trigger guard, was used to release and lock the cylinder, which had to be turned by hand. These revolvers were made in 31 caliber and had barrel lengths of 3 to 6 inches. Approximately 650 of these five shot revolvers were manufactured.[5]

In 1854 Whitney developed the Ring Trigger Pocket Revolver. Operation of this revolver required cocking the hammer and then pulling the ring trigger, which would rotate the cylinder and release the hammer. All of Colt's patents were avoided; however, the timing mechanism of this revolver was not reliable. Only about 50 of these 31 caliber revolvers were made before it was abandoned for a more reliable revolver.[6]

This next revolver was the Whitney-Beals' Patent Pocket Revolver, more commonly known as the "Walking Beam Pocket Revolver." Fordyce Beals, a gun designer and gunmaker, was hired by Whitney in 1854. He had worked for the Remington Armory prior to coming to Whitney's factory. Beals' patent number 11715, dated September 26, 1854, formed the design of this revolver. The cylinder was rotated by a three tined fork which resembled the walking beam steam engine of that period, hence the nickname of this revolver. The "Walking Beam Pocket Revolver" was made in 28 and 31 calibers. Barrel lengths varied from 2 inches to 6 inches, with a total production of about 3,200 revolvers made.[7]

Fordyce Beals returned to Remington's Armory in 1856. Whitney had certainly benefited from the services that Beals provided at Whitneyville. Whitney would soon be able to make even greater improvements to his revolvers, as Colt's patent expired in 1857. This would allow other manufacturers to produce similar revolvers that would have the same reliability. However, Colt was well ahead in the "arms race." His famous Colt 1851 Navy and 1849 Pocket Models had been in production for years and were in use world-wide. But for Whitney the timing could not have been better. The demand for personal firearms was increasing with the Westward expansion, and the American Civil War was looming on the horizon.

Whitney Two Trigger Pocket Revolver with 6 inch barrel. Serial number 20 X. Manufactured circa 1852-53.

The New York Times
Published: March 26, 1853

☞ We have had an opportunity to examine a new REPEATING PISTOL, invented by Mr. E. WHITNEY, of New Haven, Conn.; a weapon meriting more than ordinary attention. The revolving cylinder is so arranged as to be easily removed from its place and cleaned without difficulty; and a half dozen cylinders, with a half dozen charges in each, may be used in rapid succession, the substitution of a new one being the work of a moment. The advantages of the piece, are chiefly, that it does not revolve by cocking; an arrangement increasing the friction of the lock, and diminishing the size and strength of its parts; and tending to crowd the smoke of the several discharges into the cavities, and so clogging the play of the machinery. The pistol is readily loaded in the hand. The barrel is firmly applied to the cylinder; which, while it revolves upon the centre-pin, does not, as in other inventions, depend on that part for strength. The ease with which any of the mechanism may be repaired or replaced by any workman, is an additional recommendation. Of the accuracy and range of the piece we have not had an opportunity of judging. The inventor, the reader may be interested in knowing, is a son of the famous inventer of the Cotton Gin, and bears his name.

Whitneyville Armory about 1862. *(Whitney Arms Company, Van Slyck steel engraving Library of Congress)*

2

THE WHITNEY .36 CAL NAVY REVOLVER

The Whitney Navy Revolver was Eli Whitney's most successful revolver. Manufactured from the late 1850s to the mid-1860s, Whitney produced two models of this firearm, reaching a total production of approximately 35,500 revolvers. Whitney had manufactured other revolvers prior to his "Navy" model, but with the expiration of Colt's patent in 1857 he was free to produce revolvers that utilized Colt's mechanical features.

The Whitney revolver was certainly one of the first, if not the first, revolver to be manufactured with a solid frame. The barrel was octagonal and was screwed into the frame, with the screw threads visible between the frame and cylinder. The length of the barrel was listed by Whitney as 7 1/2 inches, although most that we have measured closer to 7 5/8 inches. The cylinder rotated on a "cylinder pin," rather than an "arbor," as used in Colt's revolvers. The "cylinder pin" was connected to the loading lever and rammer, which could easily be removed from the revolver by turning a "wing-nut" on the left (or sometimes right) side of the frame. This enabled the shooter to easily remove the cylinder and eliminated the need for the small "wedge" that secured the barrel to the arbor on Colt's revolvers. The sights of the Whitney Navy revolver were the brass, post-type front sight, with a rear sighting groove on the top strap of the frame. Whitney used two-piece wood grips on his revolvers.

Known as the "Belt" pistol, Whitney proclaimed his revolver to be "an improvement on Colt's, but so much like his, that all the advantages claimed for Colt's may, with equal propriety be claimed for Whitney's; and more…" In January 1860, Whitney's Price List to the Ordnance Department listed these revolvers as follows:

"BELT PISTOLS – Army and Navy, medium size, Plated mountings, six shots, 7 ½ inch barrel, caliber 36-100 of an inch (50 elongated, or 86 round bullets to the pound) with bullet mould, nipple wrench and screw-driver, - weight 2 ½ lbs…$16.80."

Whitney went on to list the improvements that made his revolver superior to Colt's.

The top bar, or jointless frame, which supercedes the necessity of securing the barrel to the cylinder and frame by means of a center-pin or arbor, and afterwards destroying it's strength by a key hole. The center-pin in any revolver should be used for the cylinder to revolve upon only, and not hold the pistol together—it is unsafe and not reliable. Whitney's revolver is a superior balanced pistol, and less subject to be diverted from the point aimed at, by the recoil, at the time of discharge."[1]

While never manufactured in the volume that Colt's revolvers were produced, the Whitney Navy Revolver was well accepted and used by the military and civilians alike. In later chapters we will examine the use of this revolver by both the Union and Confederate troops.

The Whitney Navy Revolver has been classified into two models. Within those "Models" are found several "Types". The descriptions and approximate serial number ranges for each model and type are provided in Chapter Four, and are the result of the study and analysis of 370 Whitney Navy Revolvers.

Collectors will be interested in the various changes that occurred in these revolvers, resulting in the various "type" designations. Serial number ranges have been used to easily identify the "type" designation of revolvers. Anyone who has examined a Whitney Navy revolver has found that the serial numbers are not readily visible. In the remainder of this chapter the author will provide the reader with a complete description of serial number locations.

Location of Serial Numbers

Figure 1 (p 18) will provide a quick reference for locations of all serial numbers on the Whitney revolver.

The easiest number to find is the one on the loading lever. Simply open the loading lever and look on the inside rear part of the lever. The serial number under the barrel may also be visible, or often is partially visible. Once the loading lever-rammer assembly is removed the number under the barrel will be completely visible, as will the number on the cylinder pin.

The cylinder can then be removed from the frame. A serial number is also stamped on the back (or bottom) area of the cylinder. Often the numbers are found on the ratchet areas of the cylinder. A letter may be seen in one of the safety notches of the cylinder: see Figure 2. These numbers may be very difficult to see if the pistol has seen much use, and may have been completely worn off.

The same letter appears with the serial numbers on the loading lever, bottom of the barrel, and rear of the cylinder. (For instance, if the letter "Y" is found before or after the serial number on the loading lever, the same combination is seen under the barrel and on the rear of the cylinder. The cylinder pin had only the serial number, without a letter, on all examples viewed.)

The trigger guard is held in place with one screw, so the removal of this piece is a simple matter. Under the brass trigger guard the serial number will be found. Along with the number are two letters. The serial number, with the same two letters, will also be visible on the frame when the trigger guard is removed: see Figures 5 and 6.

The wooden grips are also secured by a single screw. Once removed, the revolver's serial number should be revealed stamped on the inside of each grip. The right grip will normally have the same two letters that were found on the frame under the trigger guard and on the inside of the trigger guard. On earlier models, at approximately serial number 1000 and below, only one letter is found in these locations. On some later models, the grips may have only one of the two letters that are on the trigger guard and frame. Occasionally grips have been found with only the serial numbers and no letters.

Serial numbers may be found in the following locations:

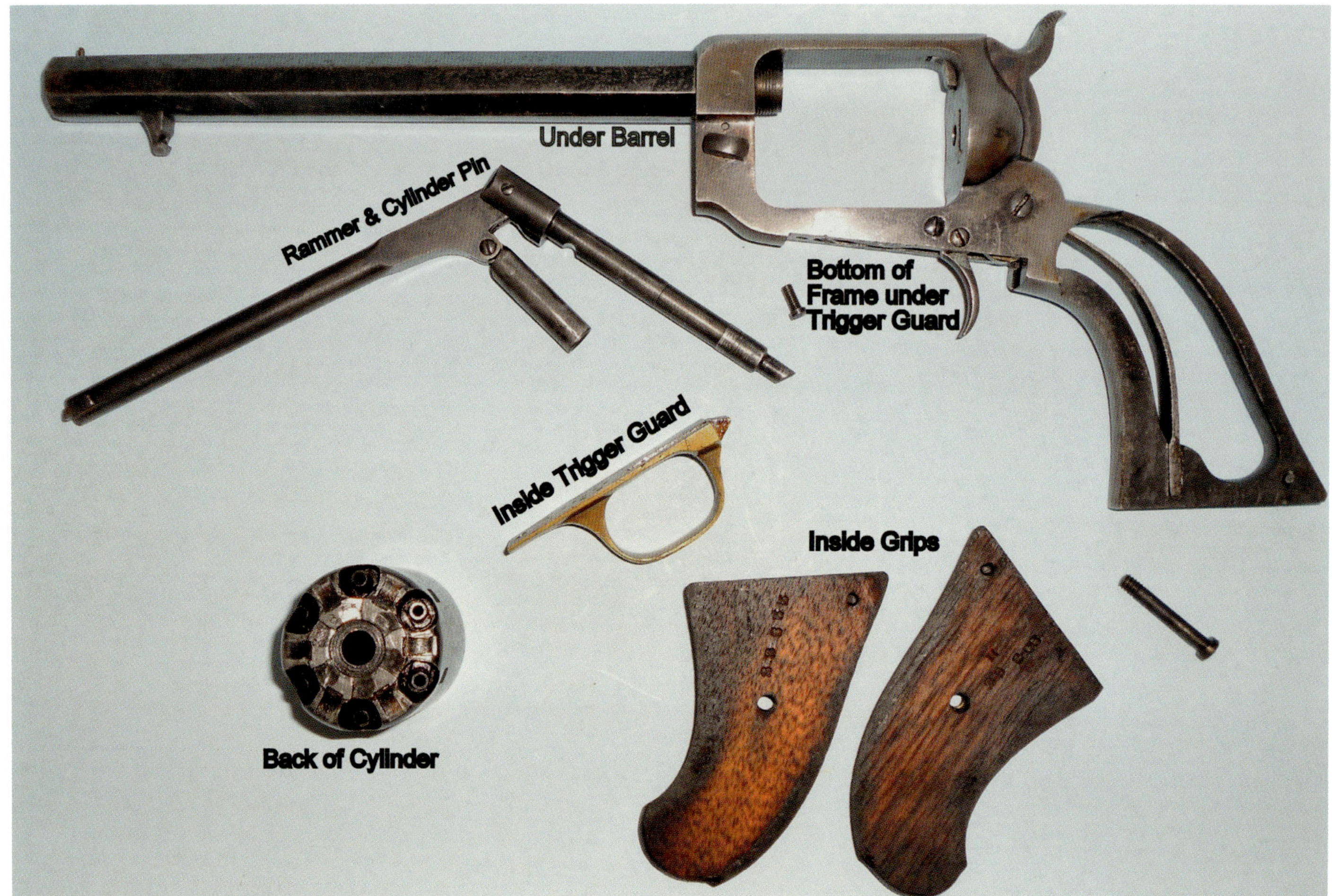

Fig. 1: *(Author's collection)*

Serial numbers are stamped on the rear of the cylinder. Revolvers that have been well used may have numbers that are only partially visible, or perhaps totally worn away. In the following example, the letter "Y" may be seen inside one of the safety slots.

Fig. 2: Serial number on back of cylinder. A letter is normally found in one safety notch. *(Author's collection)*

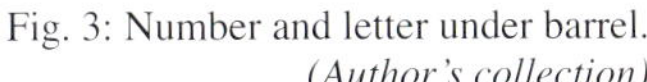

Fig. 3: Number and letter under barrel. *(Author's collection)*

Serial numbers will also be found on the loading lever and cylinder pin, inside the trigger guard, and on the frame under the trigger guard.

Fig. 4: Serial numbers are found on the cylinder pin and loading lever. Often a letter will also be seen on the loading lever. *(Author's collection)*

Fig. 5: Serial number and letters inside Trigger Guard. *(Author's collection)*

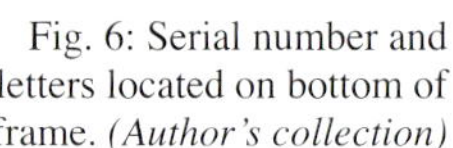
Fig. 6: Serial number and letters located on bottom of frame. *(Author's collection)*

An Analysis of the Letters found with Serial Numbers

The letters found on Whitney revolvers are thought to be assembly markings, rather than the initials of a worker. An analysis of the letters found with the serial numbers on the revolver was conducted by the author with the following observations.

The same letter is found on the barrel, loading lever, and cylinder. The following letters were frequently noted: A, C, L, K, M, O, S, Y, and X. The letters F, G, V, and Z were also noted.

Two letters are found with the serial numbers located under the trigger guard, on the frame under the trigger guard, and on the inside of the right grip. These letters were originally thought to be the initials of an inspector; however, an interesting trend developed from the analysis of the survey database. Almost without exception, the first of these two letters will progress up the alphabet as the serial numbers increase. For instance, for the 1300-2900 serial ranges the letters noted were BA, BB, BC, BJ, BE, and BS. In the 3000-4800 range they were CC, CS, CU, CV, and CX. In the 14000-16000 range JM, JO, JE, and JY. And lastly, in the 30000-32000 ranges the letters are TX, TO, TZ, UW, and UR. It appears these may be some type of batch or assembly codes. This progression of two letters was first noted with Second Model, 1st Type revolvers beginning around the 1000 serial range. Earlier revolvers with three digit serial numbers were noted to have only one letter, such as serial #159 I or #754 M.

The classification of Whitney Navy revolvers by model and type, along with their respective serial number ranges, will be covered in Chapter Four. Before proceeding to that chapter, we will review a few of the basic features and terminologies that will be mentioned throughout this book.

Fig. 7: A completely disassembled Whitney Navy revolver. (*Courtesy George Tondryk*)

3

FEATURES OF THE WHITNEY NAVY REVOLVER

As the collector examines various Whitney Navy Revolvers he will note differences in the styles of loading levers and catches, safety notches on the cylinder, cylinder scenes (if fortunate enough to find one with a visible scene), size of the trigger guard, placement of the "wing-nut," and the type of sights. Some of these key features or characteristics are used to classify a revolver into a specific "Type." There are also some characteristics that may not be as noticeable, such as the rifling and barrel address. These features are discussed, and in some cases pictured, below.

Loading Levers and Catches

There are two distinct types of loading levers and catches used on the Whitney Navy Revolvers. The earliest type was the "Ball-style" lever and catch: see Figure 1 below. This style first appeared on the First Model Whitney revolvers when loading levers were added. The "Ball-style" lever and catch continued to be used on Second Model Whitney revolvers until approximately serial number 6000.

Fig. 1: Loading levers were added at approximately serial number 100 of the First Model. The first style loading lever catches were the "Ball-type," as shown above. *(Author's collection)*

The "Colt-style" loading lever catch was a more secure and sturdy method of locking the rammer in place. See Figure 2 below. It may have been that Whitney adopted this change as part of his continuous improvement process, or perhaps this was a required change in order to secure government contracts. Regardless of the reason, the "Colt-style" lever and catch began to appear at approximately serial number 6000. A few "Ball-type" levers and catches are found intermittently in the 6000 serial number range as Whitney transitioned to the "Colt-style" lever and catch.

Fig. 2: The "Colt-style" catch provided a sturdy and more secure method of holding the loading lever in place. This transition occurred in the 6000 serial number range. *(Author's collection)*

Cylinder Safety Notches

One safety notch was added to the cylinders at approximately serial number 1000 of the First Model. Our survey found the single safety notch used as high as serial number 1977 of the Second Model, and one was reported in the 2000 range. The earliest revolver in our survey with six safety notches was serial number 2092. There may have been a transition period, somewhere around the 2000-2100 range, when six safety notches began appearing on the Whitney cylinders.

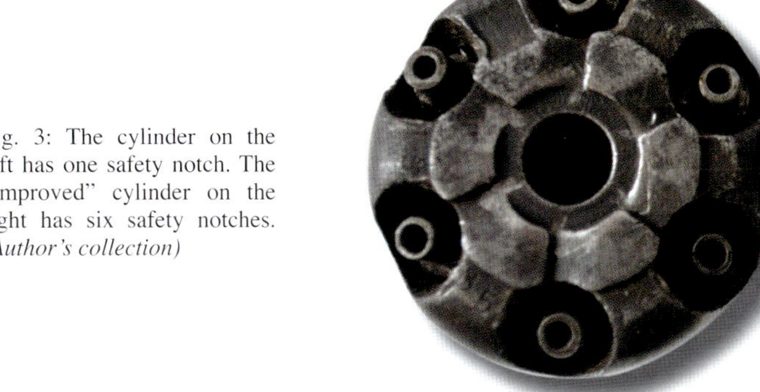

Fig. 3: The cylinder on the left has one safety notch. The "improved" cylinder on the right has six safety notches. *(Author's collection)*

Cylinder Scene

Cylinder scenes were lightly rolled, and are often seen faintly or not at all. Most of the revolvers in this survey had cylinder scenes that were no longer visible, or had only traces of a scene. If one does not know what scene was used on the Whitney revolver, one would find it nearly impossible to determine what those "traces" represented.

Of the revolvers included in this survey, approximately 17% had "good" scenes.

There are two styles of cylinder scenes:

First style: A shield (half of which is the U.S. Stars & Stripes Coat of Arms, and half the English Coat of Arms) with an Eagle on one side and a Lion on the other. This scene covered one half of the cylinder and was repeated on the opposite side of the cylinder.

Fig. 4: Eagle. *(Author's collection)*

Fig. 5: Shield with Coats of Arms. *(Author's collection)*

Fig. 6: Lion. *(Author's collection)*

The shield used by Whitney for his cylinder scenes represents a connection between the United States and England. Half of the Coat of Arms is the Stars and Stripes of the United States, and the other half is the Royal Coat of Arms of the United Kingdom. The Royal Coat of Arms, as it has appeared since 1837, is shown at right.

Fig. 7: The three lions represent England; the single lion represents Scotland; and the Harp represents Ireland. *(Courtesy of Collectors Centre Online, North Yorkshire, UK)*

The three lions represent England, the single lion represents Scotland, and the Harp represents Ireland.

On the Whitney cylinder scene, the American Eagle and the Trafalgar Lion flank the Coat of Arms. Why Whitney chose this design for his revolvers remains a mystery. The author believes this design may have been developed with the idea of marketing revolvers to England. The use of the Royal Coat of Arms and Trafalgar Lion would appeal to the English market. Colt had closed his London factory in 1857, so perhaps Whitney felt he had an opportunity to compete in that market as well.

Second style: Shield with a ribbon marked "Whitneyville" and a naval scene (with wooden ships and iron clad monitor) covered one half of the cylinder, with the original eagle, shield (with the Coats of Arms), and lion remaining on the other half of the cylinder.

One side of the cylinder remained unchanged.

The second eagle – Coat of Arms – lion, found on the opposite side of the cylinder, was replaced by the following naval scene and shield with Whitneyville Ribbon shown in Figures 11, 12, and 13 below. This consisted of a fortress with naval ships in the foreground, an ironclad monitor, and a shield with a Whitneyville ribbon draped across it.

Fig. 8: Eagle. (*Author's collection*)

Fig. 9: Coat of Arms. (*Author's collection*)

Fig. 10: Lion. (*Author's collection*)

Opposite Side of Cylinder

As the USS *Monitor* (or similar ironclad) is shown, this scene would have occurred after the introduction of ironclads in March 1862.

This style cylinder scene was first noted on a revolver in the mid-11000 serial number range. The use of this scene may have occurred even earlier. Claude Fuller, in his book *The Whitney Firearms*, describes revolver number 9003 M as having a cylinder with a "coat of arms and a naval scene."[1] Due to the difficulty in locating revolvers with clear cylinder scenes, the author was unable to verify this style scene below the 11000 serial number range.

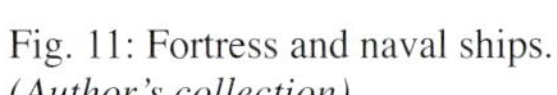

Fig. 11: Fortress and naval ships. (*Author's collection*)

Fig. 12: Iron clad monitor. (*Author's collection*)

Fig. 13: Shield with Whitneyville ribbon. (*Author's collection*)

Barrel Addresses

Three types of barrel addresses were noted:

1. EAGLE CO.
2. E. WHITNEY / N. HAVEN
3. E. WHITNEY / *N. HAVEN*

The "Eagle Co." address is found on some of the First Model Whitney Navy Revolvers. It is thought to be on those revolvers in the serial number range of 500 to approximately 1500 of the First Model. Some "E. Whitney/N. Haven" addresses were known to occur before and after the use of the "Eagle Co." address. The reason for using this address is unknown. One theory is that Whitney used it as a trade name for his more fragile revolvers while he was working on an improved version.[2]

Fig. 14: *(Photo courtesy of James D. Julia Auctioneers)*

The most frequently seen address is that of "E. WHITNEY / N. HAVEN." All Second Model revolvers carried a form of this address. A change in the style of address die was noted to have occurred slightly below serial number 13000. After that point a "slanted" *N. HAVEN* was used. Examples are shown in Figures 15 and 16.

E. WHITNEY / N. HAVEN

The earlier type "Whitney" address has block-style letters. This style address was noted on the Second Model Whitney until approximately serial number 13000.

Fig. 15: *(Author's collection)*

E. WHITNEY / *N. HAVEN*

The later type address is seen with a block-style "E. WHITNEY" and a slanted "*N. HAVEN*." The earliest revolver found with this style barrel address was serial number 12509. *There was a transition period in which the old style address was occasionally seen until approximately number 13000. After that point all barrel addresses were the new style.*

Fig. 16: *(Author's collection)*

Barrel Length

The average barrel length noted in the study was 7 5/8 inches. Whitney listed his Navy revolvers as having 7 1/2 inch barrels. His price list of January 1860 listed various barrel lengths for his Pocket Pistol, but no optional barrel lengths for the Navy revolver. The author's study found nine revolvers with short barrels, varying in length from 4 inches to 6 3/4 inches. Most of these appeared to have been cut down after leaving the factory. Only a couple appeared to have been professionally done, and could have been special orders. However, both of those revolvers also carried Naval inspection markings, which may make it doubtful that they left the factory in that manner.

Fig. 17: Wing-nut may be on left or right of frame. (*Author's collection*)

Wing-Nut

The "Wing-Nut" is fastened to a screw that runs completely through the frame, and is used to secure the cylinder pin in place. The wing-nut serves as an easy method to loosen the cylinder pin, thus allowing the pin and loading lever assembly to be removed. The cylinder may then be easily removed for cleaning. Once the cylinder and cylinder pin are replaced, the wing-nut is simply turned a half turn, locking the cylinder pin in place.

The wing-nut first appeared on Second Model Whitney revolvers. The earliest revolvers in our survey that had the wing-nut were Second Models, serial numbers 152 and 159. These earlier revolvers had small wing-nuts. See Figure 18. The larger, more common version appeared shortly thereafter. This provided for a better grip on the wing-nut and made it more user friendly. The next earliest revolver in the survey was in the 300 serial range, and featured the larger version wing-nut.

An "O" was noted on one side of the wing-nut and a similar "O" on the left side of the frame, just above where the wing-nut is located. The "O" represents "Open," rather than being the initial of an inspector. When the "O" side of the wing-nut is facing the "O" on the frame, the cylinder pin can be removed. Since the "O" on the frame is always found on the left side, it is logical that it was meant for the wing-nut to also be on the left. Those found on the right were perhaps moved for personal preference, and were found intermittently in all Types of the Second Model. There were also several revolvers noted that had the wing-nut removed and replaced with a screw.

Fig. 18: Early style wing-nut was smaller, and thinner, than the later versions. (*Author's collection*)

This revolver, serial number 21196, features a modified "wing-nut screw" that is easily removed in order to remove the cylinder pin and loading lever assembly. This is one example of a modification made to Whitney's "wing-nut" feature after leaving the factory. *(Courtesy of William Willis)*

Fig. 19: Standard Size Trigger Guard. *(Author's collection)*

Trigger Guard

Trigger guards are found in three primary types. The earliest type trigger guards were made of iron. This is the type that is found on the First Model Whitney Navy revolvers. Brass became the standard for trigger guards of the Second Model Whitney. The trigger guard was changed to a larger, brass type guard at approximately serial number 28000. The larger guard was a recommendation of the Navy Department, as noted in Chapter Five, *Martial Whitneys*.

Silvering was noted on the brass trigger guards throughout the Second Model serial range. In his price list submitted to the Ordnance Department dated January 1860, Whitney offers his pistols with "plated mountings" (See Chapter Five, *Martial Whitneys*). However, silvering was not frequently encountered in the study, and the author cannot confirm that all brass trigger guards were silver plated. Our survey indicated approximately 11% of the Second Model Whitney revolvers had silver or a remnant of silver remaining on the trigger guards. Many of the earlier revolvers were sold on the civilian market, and were possibly furnished with silvering on the guards. Like many other revolvers of the period, the silver would wear off with use. The military contracts would not have specified silvered trigger guards. Whitney's letter to the Navy dated January 28, 1863, (see Chapter Five) indicates he was not plating the trigger guards or varnishing the stocks of revolvers sold to the Army.

Fig. 20: Large Trigger Guard. *(Courtesy Darrel Favrhow)*

Sights

The standard sight arrangement for the Whitney Navy Revolver was a brass post or cone shaped front sight. The rear sight was the slot/groove in the top face of the hammer that lined up with the groove in the top of the frame and front sight. See Figures 21 and 21a, below.

Occasionally different styles of front sights were noted, including blade and dovetailed sights. These were most likely modifications made after the revolver left the factory. See Figure 22 and 22a, below.

A wedge-type front sight was noted on several revolvers. These sights may have been replacement sights for worn post sights. Two of the revolvers we noted with these wedge-type sights were martial revolvers. See Figures 23 and 24.

Fig. 21: *(Author's collection)*

Figure 21a: *(Author's collection)*

Fig. 22: *(Courtesy of Stephen Burgess – Campsite Artifacts)*

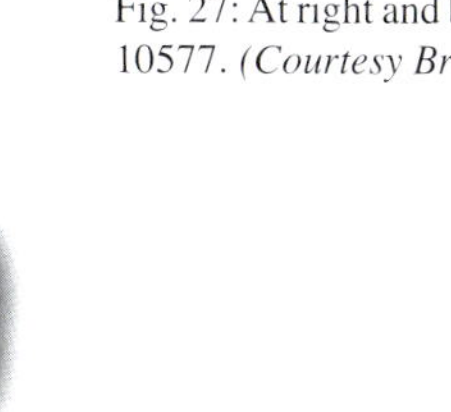

Fig. 27: At right and below: Serial number 10577. *(Courtesy Brian Santor)*

Figure 22a: *(Courtesy Brian Santor)*

A few revolvers in the survey had a blade sight, as shown in Figures 25 and 26. The sight in Figure 25 has a low or worn profile, while the other is more pronounced.

Sometimes a rear sight, added by a competent gunsmith, may be found, as seen on the revolver shown in Figure 27 on the previous page (the dovetailed front sight of this revolver is shown in Figure 22a).

Fig. 23: Serial number 19163. *(Courtesy of Eli Whitney Museum)*

Fig. 24: Serial number 13060. *(Courtesy of William Henry Lee)*

Fig. 25: Serial number 6792. *(Courtesy of Eli Whitney Museum)*

Fig. 26: Serial number 32451. *(Courtesy Darrel Favrhow)*

Rifling

Two types of rifling were used in the barrels of Whitney Navy revolvers. Seven grooves and lands are seen in most of the Whitney revolvers encountered. This seems to have been the standard used by Whitney and other manufacturers during this era. There were several revolvers in the study that were noted as having "five-groove" rifling. The earliest serial number noted was 25127; however, many of the subsequent revolvers had seven-groove rifling. Revolvers with five-groove rifling were also noted in the 26000, 30000, and 32000 ranges, with seven-groove rifling continuing to be found frequently in these ranges. The highest numbered revolver in this study was 32862, and was reported as having seven rifling grooves.

The various Models and Types of Whitney Navy revolvers will be discussed in Chapter Four. The author has elected not to use the number of rifling grooves as a change in revolver design, since the use of five-groove rifling was found inconsistently in both the 4th and 5th Types of the Second Model.

Fig. 28: The revolver on the left has 5 grooves, while the one on the right has 7 grooves. The wider grooves may be noted on the muzzle of the revolver on the left. *(Courtesy Marc & Dan Williams)*

(Courtesy The Whitney Library, The New Haven Museum)

4

CLASSIFICATION OF THE WHITNEY NAVY REVOLVER BY MODEL AND TYPE

In this chapter the author will list the descriptive features of the various models and types of the Whitney Navy Revolver that resulted from this Study.

Several very nice examples of First Model Whitney Navy revolvers were located during the author's research; however, the number of revolvers found was very limited. The following photographs will provide examples of revolvers in each of the various types.

First Model

All of the First Model Whitney Navy revolvers were noted to have iron trigger guards. There are four types of the First Model revolver, as listed below. Each type following the "1st Type" will have the same features as the preceding type, unless changes are noted. Additional, or new, features are indicated for each type following the 1st Type.

1st Type (*Approximate serial number range* 1-100)

Light construction; thin top strap; no loading lever assembly; iron trigger guard; square juncture of grips; 4-screw frame. No barrel markings. Address markings may or may not be present on top of frame.

Cylinder scene: eagle, shield and lion.

First Model, 1st Type Whitney. Serial number 23

Fig. 1: First Model Whitney Revolver Serial No. 23 with variant cylinder pin. Thin top strap. No cylinder notches. There are no markings on this revolver except the serial number. The serial number is found on the butt and on the insides of each grip. There are no address markings on top of the frame or barrel. *(Courtesy of The Hayes Otoupalik Collection. Photo by: Darin Deyo)*

Fig. 2: First Model, 1st Type Whitney. Serial number 23. *(Courtesy of The Hayes Otoupalik Collection. Photo by: Darin Deyo)*

Another First Model, serial #2, was noted as being marked "ADDRESS E. WHITNEY / WHITNEYVILLE. CT." on top of the frame. This address is similar to the address Whitney used on some of his first revolvers in the early1850s.

A similar First Model, 1st Type revolver is pictured in *The Whitney Firearms* by Claud E. Fuller. He indicates the top of the frame, rather than the barrel, is stamped "E. WHITNEY." Fuller describes the revolver as:

"the forward part of the frame is minus the customary loading grove, as it evidently was the intention to remove the cylinder for the purpose of loading. To facilitate this, the arm is provided with the spring-lever catch and cylinder pin described in E. Whitney's patent No. 11447, dated August 1, 1854, as follows:

And in the manner of using the spring-lever catch and rod or mandral with two notches to hold the chambered breech in its place, and to hold the rod from falling out while removing or changing the chambered breech."[1]

2nd Type (*Approximate serial number range* 100-300)
Attached loading lever; ball-type catch.

Two revolvers in this serial number range were surveyed. Both had barrels that were marked "E. WHITNEY / N. HAVEN". Note the 4-screw frame.

Fig. 3: First Model, 2nd Type Whitney. Serial number 131. *(Photo courtesy of James D. Julia Auctioneers)*

3rd Type (*Approximate serial number range* 300-1000)

Three-screw frame and 3-piece center-linked loading lever providing a smoother straight line operation. Above serial #500, most barrels marked EAGLE CO.

Fig. 5: Barrel Address of revolver number 605 is "EAGLE CO." *(Photo courtesy of James D. Julia Auctioneers)*

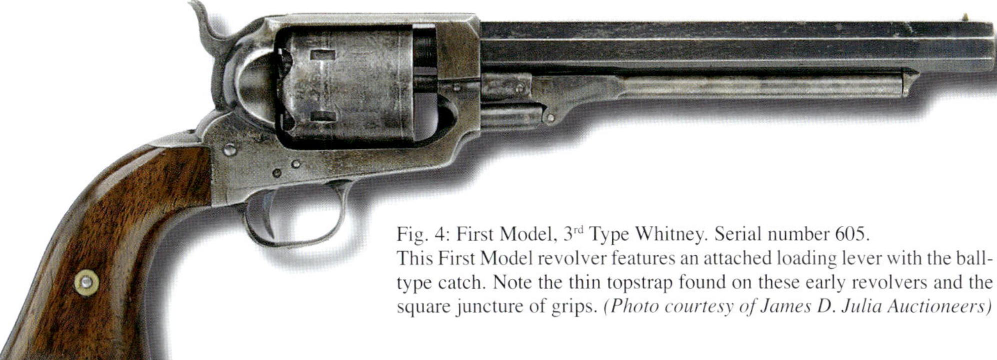

Fig. 4: First Model, 3rd Type Whitney. Serial number 605.
This First Model revolver features an attached loading lever with the ball-type catch. Note the thin topstrap found on these early revolvers and the square juncture of grips. *(Photo courtesy of James D. Julia Auctioneers)*

Fig. 6: First Model, 3rd Type Whitney. Serial number 949.
Whitney Revolver marked "Eagle Co." on barrel. Serial number 949. Grips marked with owner's name, H. NOBLE. Thin top strap, no cylinder notches for hammer. Early frame and loading lever. *(Courtesy of The Hayes Otoupalik Collection. Photo by: Darin Deyo)*

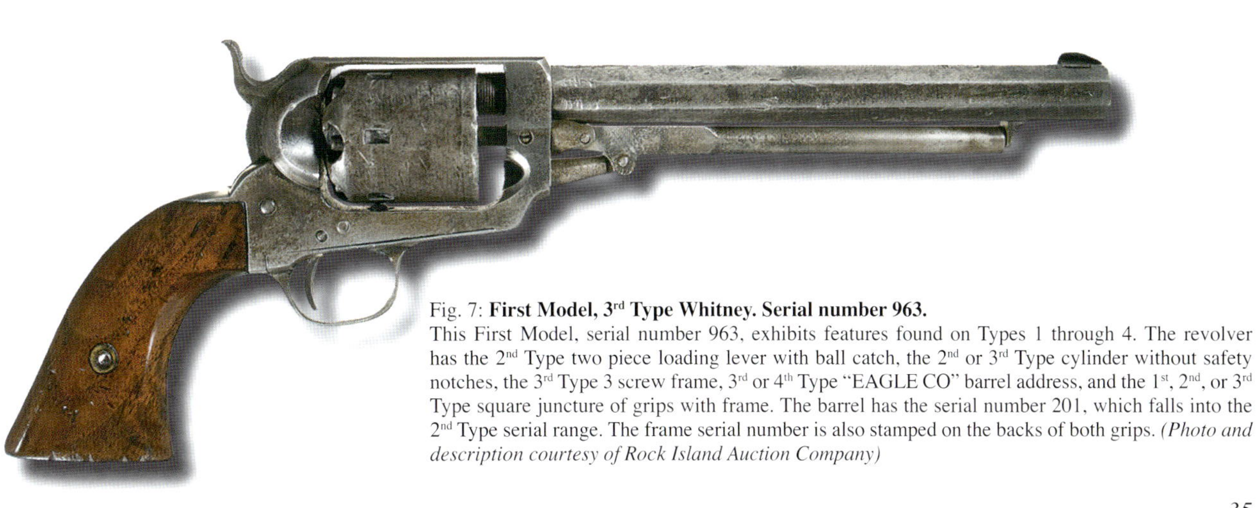

Fig. 7: **First Model, 3rd Type Whitney. Serial number 963.**
This First Model, serial number 963, exhibits features found on Types 1 through 4. The revolver has the 2nd Type two piece loading lever with ball catch, the 2nd or 3rd Type cylinder without safety notches, the 3rd Type 3 screw frame, 3rd or 4th Type "EAGLE CO" barrel address, and the 1st, 2nd, or 3rd Type square juncture of grips with frame. The barrel has the serial number 201, which falls into the 2nd Type serial range. The frame serial number is also stamped on the backs of both grips. *(Photo and description courtesy of Rock Island Auction Company)*

4th Type (*Approximate serial number range* 1000-1500)
Rounded juncture of grips to frame; one safety notch on cylinder; iron trigger guard; most barrels marked EAGLE CO.; some with E. Whitney/N. Haven.

This "Type" is very similar to the Second Model, 1st Type, having the rounded juncture of the grips to the frame and one safety notch added to the cylinder.

The distinguishing characteristics are the thin top strap, iron trigger guard, and absence of a wing nut.

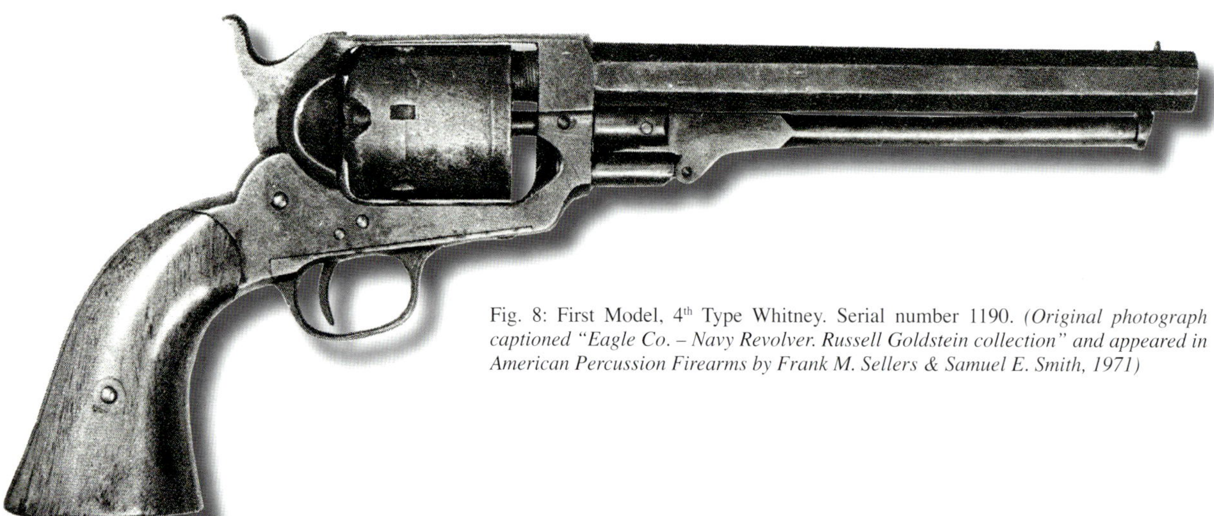

Fig. 8: First Model, 4th Type Whitney. Serial number 1190. *(Original photograph captioned "Eagle Co. – Navy Revolver. Russell Goldstein collection" and appeared in American Percussion Firearms by Frank M. Sellers & Samuel E. Smith, 1971)*

Second Model

1st Type (*Approximate serial number range* 1-2000)
Heaver, stronger frame construction; brass trigger guard; cylinder pin secured by wing-nut; one safety notch on cylinder; barrel marked E. Whitney/N. Haven. Ball-type lever catch. Cylinder scene: eagle, shield and lion.

Fig. 9: Second Model, 1st Type Whitney. Serial number 159.
A very early 1st Type revolver, serial number 159. This revolver has a small wing-nut on the left side of the frame. *(Author's collection)*

Fig. 10: Serial number "13" and "35."
Cylinder of Whitney number 1335. Note the single safety notch. *(Author's collection)*

Fig. 11: Second Model, 1st Type Whitney. Serial number 1335.
Another early 1st Type revolver, serial number 1335. This revolver has a single safety notch on the cylinder and a standard sized "wing-nut" on the left side of the frame. *(Author's collection)*

The barrel address found on the Second Model Whitney Navy Revolvers is: "E.WHITNEY / N. HAVEN."

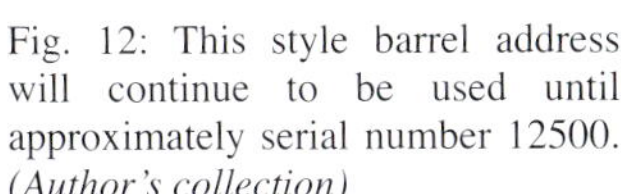

Fig. 12: This style barrel address will continue to be used until approximately serial number 12500. *(Author's collection)*

2nd Type (*Approximate serial number range* 2000-6000)
Six safety notches added to the cylinder. All other features are the same as those of the 1st Type.

Fig. 13: Second Model, 2nd Type Whitney. Serial number 5326. *(Courtesy of William Henry Lee collection)*

Fig. 14: Six safety notches on cylinder. *(Courtesy of William Henry Lee collection)*

3rd Type (*Approximate serial number range* 6000-11000)

"Colt-style" loading lever and catch appears in this range. A transition from the "ball-style" lever occurred in the early 6000 serial number range. Some "ball-type" levers may still be found intermittently in the 6000 range.

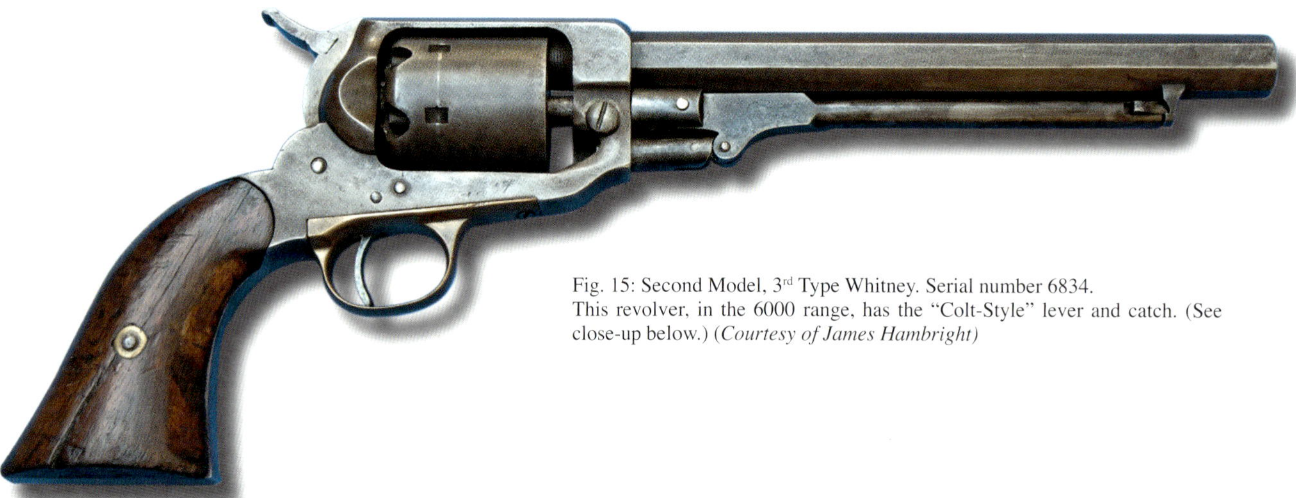

Fig. 15: Second Model, 3rd Type Whitney. Serial number 6834. This revolver, in the 6000 range, has the "Colt-Style" lever and catch. (See close-up below.) (*Courtesy of James Hambright)*

The "Colt-style" lever catch evolved during the early 6000 serial range. Some slight variations of the lever catch will be occasionally noted in the early stages of development. The style shown is found on most of the 3rd Type revolvers and throughout the remaining production of the Whitney Navy revolver.

Fig. 16: (*Courtesy of James Hambright)*

4th Type (*Approximate serial number range* 11000-28000)
Cylinder scene: eagle; lion; Coat of Arms; naval engagement and a shield bearing a ribbon marked WHITNEYVILLE. (Two styles of barrel addresses are found in the 4th Type. After about serial number 12500, the barrel address became "E. WHITNEY / N. HAVEN," in which a slanted style lettering was used in the N. HAVEN stamp.) Changes in rifling from 7 grooves to 5 grooves began to appear in revolvers of the 4th Type. The earliest serial number noted with five groove rifling was 25127; however, most revolvers continue to be found with the seven groove rifling.

Fig. 17: Second Model, 4th Type Whitney. Serial number 13060. This revolver bears Army Inspector markings and a faint cartouche. *(Courtesy of William Henry Lee collection)*

Fig. 18: Second Model, 4th Type Whitney. Serial number 24177. *(Courtesy Frank Graves)*

Changes to the cylinder scene distinguished the 4th Type revolvers.

Fig. 19: Naval scene with monitor. *(Author's collection)*

Fig. 20: Whitneyville ribbon on shield. *(Author's collection)*

Two types of barrel address styles are found on the 4th Type revolvers and are shown below.

Fig. 21: **E.WHITNEY / N.HAVEN**. *(Author's collection)*

Fig. 22: **E.WHITNEY** / ***N.HAVEN*** After about serial number 12500. *(Author's collection)*

Some Revolvers have five groove rifling.

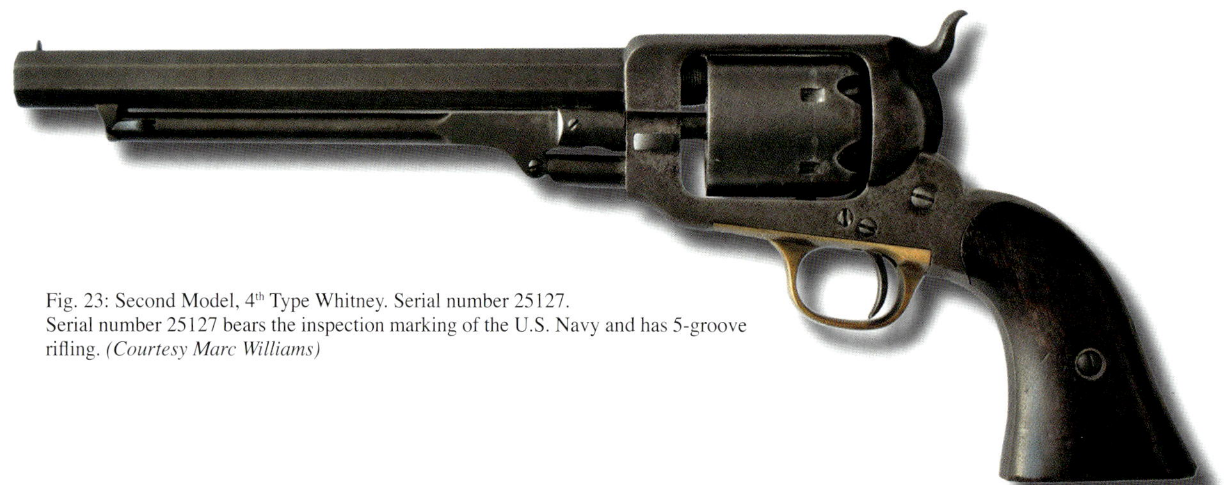

Fig. 23: Second Model, 4th Type Whitney. Serial number 25127.
Serial number 25127 bears the inspection marking of the U.S. Navy and has 5-groove rifling. *(Courtesy Marc Williams)*

5th Type (*Approximate serial number range* 28000-34000)
A large trigger guard appeared in the early 28000 range. A regular size guard may occasionally be seen in the very early 28000 range as the transition took place. Both five-groove and seven-groove barrel rifling continued to be found throughout this "type" range.

Fig. 24: Second Model, 5th Type Whitney. Serial number 28619.
Note the large trigger guard. *(Courtesy Thomas "Rusty" Van Landingham)*

Fig. 25: Second Model, 5th Type Whitney. Serial number 29630. This revolver has Seven-Groove Barrel Rifling. *(Courtesy Samantha Allison and William Heavenor)*

Fig. 26: Second Model, 5th Type Whitney. Serial number 31255. This revolver has Seven-Groove Barrel Rifling. *(Courtesy Christer Cederroth)*

Fig. 27: Second Model, 5th Type Whitney. Serial number 32451. This revolver has Five-Groove Barrel Rifling. *(Courtesy Darrel Favrhow)*

Several revolvers in the 32000 range were included in the database for this study; however, none in the 33000 range were seen. In a letter written by the late Ken Domina, he indicated that Whitney Navy revolver serial number 33874 was in his personal collection. Therefore, the Second Model serial range reached approximately 34000.

Tintype of Union soldier with Whitney Navy revolver. *(Courtesy of R.J. Askeland)*

5

MARTIAL WHITNEYS

The American Civil War provided the Whitney Arms Company a significant market for the Navy Revolver, but Eli Whitney, Jr. had to diligently pursue contracts with the Bureau of Ordnance before having his revolvers accepted. Although long experienced in the production of muskets for the government, Whitney had to be very persistent in marketing his revolvers. Just as the other arms makers of the period, he could not compete with Colt until the patent on Colt's revolver had expired. However, as the reader will see in this chapter, Whitney began to market his revolvers in the early 1850s. These were his earlier revolvers, such as the .31 caliber double trigger revolver and the Whitney-Beals Patent ring trigger revolver. Both of these were designed in such a manner so as to not infringe on Colt's patent. Whitney's Navy revolver would be in production when Colt's patent expired, and that revolver would be Whitney's most famous and successful revolver. The Whitney Navy revolvers were as good as any and better than most revolvers; however, they were never to be produced in quantities that would match those of Colt's revolvers. Colt was a master in marketing, and his revolvers were already in use throughout the United States and in Europe. By the end of the Civil War, almost 17,000 Whitney Navy Revolvers would be purchased by the Army and Navy. The author consulted *Civil War Arms Purchases & Deliveries*, by Stuart C. Mowbray, and determined there were at least 10,587 Whitney Navy revolvers purchased by the U.S. Army. Mowbray's book provides an easy reference to Executive Document No. 99, which is a congressional record of arms purchased by the Ordnance Department during the War.[1] Another 6,224 revolvers would be purchased by the US Navy. These purchases would account for approximately 50% of the 34,000 Second Model Navy revolvers that were manufactured by Whitney.

The Army purchased at least 2,193 Whitney Navy revolvers from various private sources between August 1861 and September 1863. Some of these sources included businesses, such as Schuyler, Hartley & Graham; Phillip S. Justice; and Palmer & Batchelders. These actions demonstrated the immediate need to procure arms following the Union defeat at Manassas, the first major battle of the war, in July 1861. The first purchase of revolvers directly from the Whitney Armory occurred in March 1862, with deliveries to the Army coming later that year. The Army also purchased 792 revolvers from the State of New Jersey during 1863 and 1864.

Whitney began his efforts to market revolvers to the Bureau of Ordnance as early as 1853, well before the expiration of Colt's patent. The author is indebted to two gentlemen, Ken Domina and Don Ware, whose research in the National Archives produced letters that document Whitney's efforts with the Ordnance Bureau. This author also felt that in sharing some of these letters, the reader could fully appreciate the efforts of Whitney and the quality of his Navy revolver.

In February 1853, Whitney provided the Bureau of Ordnance a quote for revolvers of four sizes: $12.00 for the three inch; $12.50 for the four inch; $13.00 for the five inch; and $13.50 for the six inch barrels. Even then he noted his revolvers were less in price than Colt's revolvers. The Bureau sent the following reply:

Bureau of Ordnance & Hydro.
February 15th, 1853

Mr. E. Whitney
New Haven, Connecticut
Sir,

Your letter of the 14th inst. has been received.

The Bureau will purchase for examination, one Repeating Pistol of each of the sizes named in your letter, and you are requested to have them sent to this Bureau, with a bill of their cost, which will be approved upon the receipt of the Pistols and their appendages in good order.

Respectfully,
Your Obt. Servt.
C. Morris, Chief of Bureau

Whitney shipped the revolvers with the following letter:

New Haven, March 30 / 53

Commdr. L [sic] *Morris*
Chief of Ordn. & Hydrography

Sir,

I send you four of my revolvers & their appendages & flasks as ordered in yours of Febry 15th ultimo, with the exception of substituting a 5 inch for the 3 inch barrel. The 3 inch barrel pistols are not the most suitable for the Navy and we make but few of them. I hope this alteration from the letter of your order will meet your approbation. I send enclosed duplicate copies of my printed list of prices to the trade by which you will see that if 100 pistols are ordered you are enabled to purchase them at a discount of 25 percent from the retail prices & if 1200 do 30 percent discount will be made.

I am selling them freely. Many prefer them to Colts tho they have been in the market but about 2 weeks. I have had one fired over 1,000 times without failure or scarcely any cleaning and it is as good for 5,000 more shots as it has been for the 1,000. It would give me pleasure to receive your further orders & to such an extent as will enable a through test of them to be made to prove their fitness for Naval service of U. States. I send the box today per express.

You will find the bill for pistols & c [etc.] *enclosed.*

Yours very respectfully,
Eli Whitney [2]

In this shipment Whitney included 1 six-inch, 2 five-inch, and 1 four-inch revolver, and 4 powder flasks for a total cost of $54.00. As these revolvers were manufactured prior to the expiration of Colt's revolving patent, it is believed that they were the "Whitney Two Trigger" revolvers. These revolvers featured the two triggers: one to lock and unlock the cylinder for rotation by hand, and a second to discharge the revolver. The Bureau purchased these four revolvers on April 5, 1853.

In 1855, Whitney sent samples of his new Whitney-Beals Revolver to the Bureau. One each of these seven shot revolvers with three, four, five, and six inch barrels were received and purchased by the Bureau on July 6, 1855. These revolvers were based on the patents of Fordyce Beals, who was later associated with E. Remington & Sons. Collectors know this model as the "Walking Beam Model" due to the peculiar cylinder revolving mechanism.[3]

Whitney attempted to sell revolvers to the Bureau again in 1857. The author found this correspondence of interest, as Colt's patent had expired.

Office of Whitneyville Armory
Whitneyville (Near New Haven, Conn.)
October 23rd, 1857

Capt. D.N. Ingraham
Chief of Bureau of Ordn. & Hydro.
Sir:

I am now ready to contract to furnish, if desired, your department with (Colt's)[4] *repeating pistols like Colts of the Navy or Belt sizes (or Army) at $12.00 each for Navies, $10.00 ea. for Belt & $15.00 for Army size. I can supply better pistols of my own new model, but with Colt's revolving attachment at the same prices. If you choose to order it I can send samples.*

Yours very respectfully
Eli Whitney

I have made near 30,000 rifles for the U.S. Govt. & have extensive and complete Machinery & c [etc.].

The first option was a copy of the Colt Model 1851 Navy. According to Flayderman's *Guide to Antique American Firearms*, approximately 300-400 of these revolvers were made from 1857-1858. Whether Whitney used surplus Colt parts or completely fabricated the revolver is unknown. It differed from Colt's 1851 Navy, in that it had two-piece walnut grips, no barrel address, and the Whitney cylinder scene consisting of an eagle, shield, and lion. One of these revolvers is pictured on page 288 in the book *Civil War Guns* by William B. Edwards. The above information was unknown when Edwards' book was published. Edwards indicates this revolver is in the Colt Museum and has serial number 302 stamped upside down on the usual parts. The same picture of this revolver may be seen on page 216 in the book *'51 Colt Navies* by Nathan Swayze.

The second option, "my own *New Model*," was an early Whitney Navy Model. This was probably a First Model, having the cylinder revolving mechanism similar to the Colt. Colt's patent had expired, and the Whitney Navy Model was making its appearance.

No evidence was found to show that the Bureau purchased either of these revolvers. A month later Whitney contacted the Bureau again to offer them 250-300 Colt Navy pistols. It is speculated that these revolvers were actually Colt Model 1851 "Navys" that had been issued to State militias and were resold by them to Whitney.[5] The Bureau again turned down Whitney's offer, stating that "this Bureau does not desire to make any purchases of Colt's pistols for the use of the Navy."

In January 1858, Whitney made a personal visit to Washington to deliver one of the Colt Navy revolvers for evaluation. Whitney stated in a letter to Captain D.N. Ingraham, Chief of Bureau of Ordnance, dated February 17, 1858, that he had "sold the 300 Colts pistols I offered your Dept. at $15. ea. I can however make as good or better pistols at same rate with frame like his or mine. Like mine at $12. ea." Again, no orders resulted. Whitney was apparently trying to persuade the Navy by offering either Colt Navy pistols or his own "New Model." He again sent a sample Colt Navy revolver to the Bureau of Ordnance on February 28, 1858, stating that he was sending "a sample of Colts Navy pistol such as I am willing to make provided a sufficient number are given to manufacture. I will make them from $15. ea. to $12. ea. according to quantity required." He then added, "I will send you another sample pistol soon with top bar similar to the one I showed you when in Washington."[6] These letters indicate that Whitney's First Model Navy revolvers (with the Whitney frame and top bar) were in production by late 1857 and early 1858.

In 1859, Whitney persuaded the Bureau to test another one of his revolvers, followed by this letter of advice regarding the test:

Office of Whitneyville Armory
Whitneyville, Conn. June 16th, 1859

Capt. Ingraham
Chief of Ord. & Hud.

Sir,

If the Officer will tallow or put oil on top of the balls in firing my pistol it will prevent the balls from leading. Please caution the officer who tries my pistol to be careful in the use of it as it is to be used as a model by my men to manufacture after.

Yours Very Respectfully,
Eli Whitney[7]

This letter implies Whitney had sent a new model, that was not yet being manufactured, to the Navy for testing. Perhaps the Second Model revolvers were in the early stages of development.

However, as the following letters indicate, his revolver did not pass the test:

Bureau of Ordnance & Hydro.
June 17th, 1859

E. Whitney Esq.
Whitneyville, Connecticut

Sir,

Herewith you will receive copy of Commander Dahlgrens report of trial made at the Navy Yard, Washington of one of your revolvers, from which you will perceive that the arm has not stood the test which was expected.

The box containing two revolvers sent by you to this Bureau will be returned today by Adams Express.

Very Respectfully,
D.N. Ingraham, Chief of the Bureau

Ordnance Office, U.S. Navy Yard
Washington, June 16th, 1859

Captain Ingraham
Chief of Bureau of Ordnance & Hydro.

Sir:

Conformable to your verbal directions, I submitted to the test of firing the revolver you handed me (Whitney's).

After the 84th fire (14 cylinders) it ceased to work efficiently, and I return it herewith for your inspection.

You will perceive that the hammer frequently fails to stay at full cock.

I have the honor to be very respectfully,
Your Obedient Servant,
John A. Dahlgren
Commander in Charge of Ordnance Department[8]

Whitney again approached the Bureau shortly after the beginning of the Civil War in an effort to sell his revolvers. He was advised that there were sufficient revolvers on hand for the present emergency, even though the Bureau was ordering revolvers from Colt. The Army and Navy seemed to be complacent regarding the arms situation during the early months of the war; however, that would soon change.

The price list on the following page was submitted to the U.S. Ordnance Department in January 1860, soliciting purchase of Whitney's Revolvers.

The Whitney Navy revolver pictured below was carried by Col Julius Adams, USMA, during the Civil War.

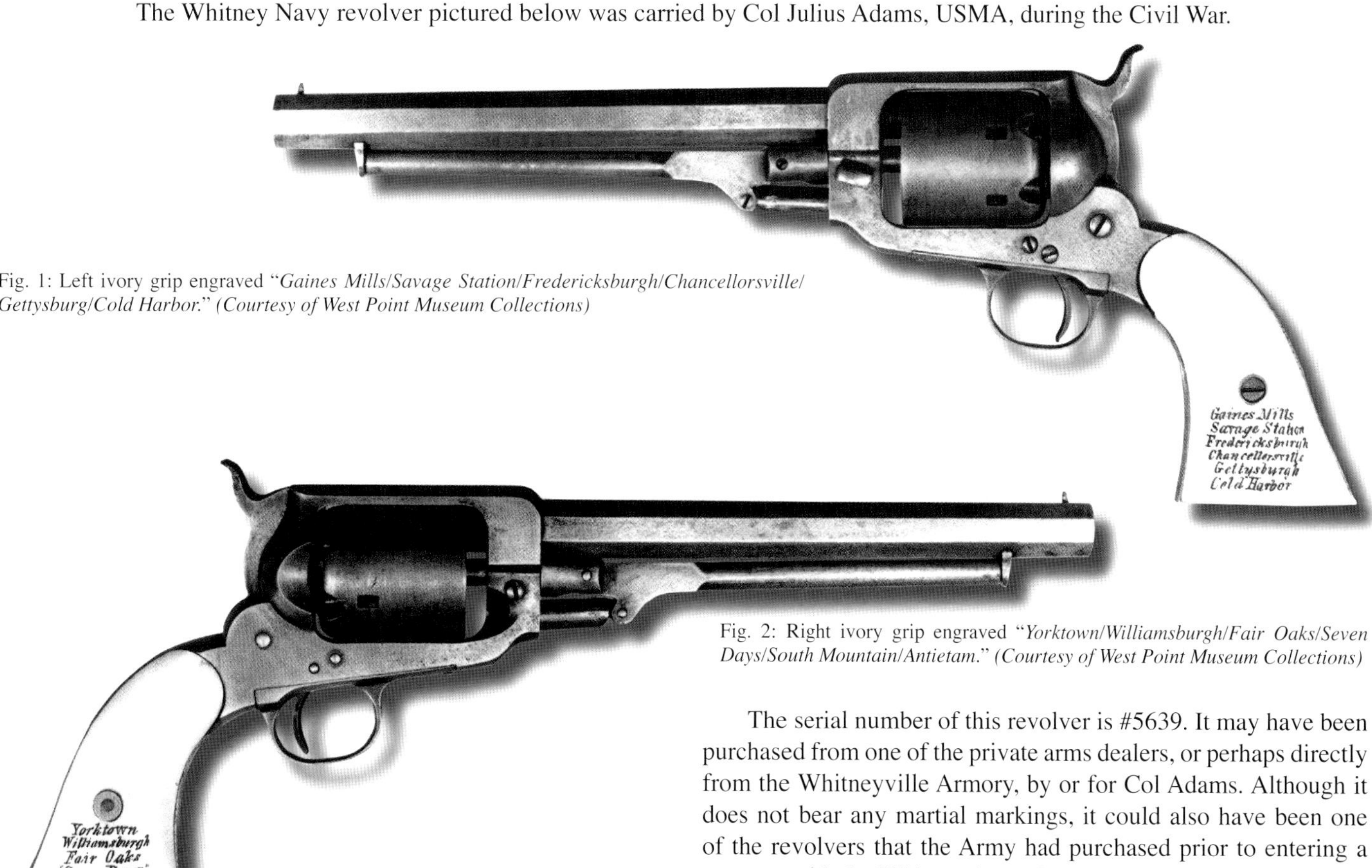

Fig. 1: Left ivory grip engraved "*Gaines Mills/Savage Station/Fredericksburgh/Chancellorsville/ Gettysburg/Cold Harbor.*" *(Courtesy of West Point Museum Collections)*

Fig. 2: Right ivory grip engraved "*Yorktown/Williamsburgh/Fair Oaks/Seven Days/South Mountain/Antietam.*" *(Courtesy of West Point Museum Collections)*

The serial number of this revolver is #5639. It may have been purchased from one of the private arms dealers, or perhaps directly from the Whitneyville Armory, by or for Col Adams. Although it does not bear any martial markings, it could also have been one of the revolvers that the Army had purchased prior to entering a contract with the Whitney Arms Company.

Price List from Eli Whitney to Ordnance Department, January 1860.

Office of Whitneyville Armory.

SIR:

WHITNEY'S REPEATING PISTOL

Is an improvement on Colt's, but so much like his, that all the advantages claimed for Colt's, may, with equal propriety be claimed for Whitney's; and more—calibres being the same—while the price is very much less. Be sure and examine Whitney's pistol, and ascertain price, before purchasing elsewhere.

The improvements consist in the top bar, or jointless frame, which supercedes the necessity of securing the Barrel to the Cylinder and Frame by means of a Center-pin or Arbor, and afterwards destroying its strength by a key hole. The Center-pin in any Revolver should be used for the Cylinder to revolve upon only, and not to hold the Pistol together—it is unsafe and not reliable. Whitney's Revolver is a superior balanced pistol, and less subject to be diverted from the point aimed at, by the recoil, at the time of its discharge. The principal weight lies in the Breech and Cylinder, and hence rests better on the hand than if the weight, or a large portion of it, was between the Muzzle and the Cylinder, or the hand.

Whitney's Revolvers are equal to any in market. They are made of the best materials, and in a superior manner. Besides being better balanced, they are more accurate shooters than the old style Repeating Pistols, most in use, because the barrel is more firmly held to the Cylinder, so that there is no yielding, or springing apart, when the ball leaves the cylinder to slug through the barrel. Whitney's Pistols are warranted safe in all respects, efficient, and durable, if properly used. These Pistols are offered in market at less price than those now most in use, not from any inferiority, but simply from the fact that the manufacturer's expenses are less than many others', since he operates his extensive Armory at Whitneyville, Conn.,—full of accurate and expensive machinery—by water-power, instead of steam; and that he is satisfied with a moderate profit, being ready at all times to share his profit with the trade. Colt's Patent, of most consequence to the public, expired in 1857, and what has been said in favor of that arm in the numerous trials it has undergone, can with equal truth be said in favor of Whitney's, as the latter is in a great measure modelled after Colt's Pistol, avoiding its gross defects. It is so much like Colt's Pistol, that it is usually called by the trade, Whitney's Colt's Pistol. There is nothing to prevent making a pistol almost precisely like Colt's: but the subscriber being a manufacturer of long experience in fire arms, and having once made 1,000 Colt's Pistols for the United States Government, prefers his own model, as more scientific in construction, and for the above-mentioned advantages and improvements, and on account of its having a better distribution of material.

PRICES.

POCKET PISTOL.—Plated mountings, five shots, 31-100 of an inch Calibre, (92 elongated, or 140 round bullets to the pound,) with Bullet Mould, Nipple Wrench and Screw-driver.

3½ inch Barrel, weight 23 oz.	$9.00
4 " " " 24 oz.	10.00
5 " " " 25½ oz.	11.00
6 " " " 27 oz.	12.00

BELT PISTOLS.—Army and Navy, medium size, Plated mountings, six shots, 7½ inch Barrel, Calibre 36-100 of an inch, (50 elongated, or 86 round bullets to the pound,) with Bullet Mould, Nipple Wrench and Screw-driver,—weight 2½ lbs. $16.80

NEW MODEL POCKET PISTOL.—Steel mountings, five shots, 3½ inch Barrel, Calibre 265-1000 of an inch, (128 elongated, or 200 round bullets to the pound,) with Bullet Mould, Nipple Wrench and Screw-driver,—weight 14 oz. $9.00

Ornamental engraving on Pocket Pistols, extra,	4.00
" " on Belt and Holster Pistols, extra,	5.00
Ivory Stock for Pocket Pistol, extra,	5.00
" " " Belt and Holster Pistol, extra,	6.00
Powder Flask for Holster Pistol, extra,	1.25
" " " Belt " "	1.00
" " " Pocket and New Model Pistol, extra,	.50

LIBERAL DISCOUNTS TO THE TRADE.

The subscriber has made nearly 30,000 Rifles for the United States Government, and for the manner in which they were made, let the following letter from the Hon. JEFFERSON DAVIS, U. S. Senator, (late Secretary of War, and Colonel of the First Regiment Mississippi Riflemen, in the Mexican war,) dated Nov. 7th, 1847; and addressed to the United States Ordnance Office, testify:

"The fine Rifles you issued to the Regiment I had the honor to command in Mexico, are worthy of the highest commendations. I doubt whether as many pieces were ever issued from any other Ordnance Department so *perfect* in their *construction* and *condition*. In *accuracy* of fire, they are *equal to the finest* SPORTING RIFLES; their range, I think, exceeds that of the old pattern Musket, and they less often miss fire, or want repair, than any small arm I have ever seen used in service."

Signed,

JEFFERSON DAVIS, *ex-Col. Mississippi Riflemen.*

Use *soft* lead for balls, and put some grease or tallow on top of the balls when in the cylinder, before the pistol is discharged. This Prevents leading the barrel.

For further information with regard to the above, and also with regard to Mississippi and Minnie Rifles, and Muskets, and Flint-Lock Muskets, if wanted, address,

Yours, respectfully,

ELI WHITNEY,

WHITNEYVILLE, CONN., U. S. A.

January, 1860.

Fig. 3: An interesting note to the above request is the endorsement of Jefferson Davis, ex. Col. Mississippi Riflemen. Davis was a U.S. Senator in 1860, and was also a former Secretary of War. The following year, he would resign from the senate when his state seceded from the Union, and within a month of that resignation, Davis would become President of the Confederate States of America. *(Courtesy Texas Governor Sam Houston records. Archives and Information Services Division, Texas State Library and Archives Commission)*

Following the First Battle of Manassas in 1861, the complacent attitude of the Bureau of Ordnance changed. Even though he still had no contract for his revolvers, Whitney was successful in furnishing thousands of muskets to the Bureau.

In 1861, the Army procured at least 1,281 Whitney revolvers from private sources. A total of 2,985 revolvers were obtained from private sources (including 792 from the State of New Jersey) during the War.[9]

In June 1862, Whitney received a contract from the Army Ordnance Department for six thousand Navy revolvers. Five thousand of these had been delivered by January 1863. However, by 1863 the Army was interested in obtaining contracts for .44 caliber revolvers, and its contract with Whitney was not renewed. So, in January 1863 Whitney once again submitted his revolvers to the Bureau, seeking a contract with the Navy:

Office of Whitneyville Armory, established in 1800
Whitneyville (Near New Haven, Conn.)
January 28, 1863

Captain J.A. Dahlgren
Chief of Ordnance, Washington
Sir:

The 100 Navy Muskets are inspected and boxed awaiting your orders where to send them. The inspector has commenced another lot of muskets.

I have taken the liberty of sending to your address a small box by express containing six Navy size .36 calibre revolving pistols as a sample of what I am making at the rate of 1,000 per month for the War Dept. They are inspected in the regular way according to Army Regulations.

I will thank you to do me the favor to have them tried in such a manner as you may think proper to test their serviceability and efficiency and if they prove to be such as your Dept. requires, I should be happy to receive an order for a few thousand for the low price of $12. each, being the same that I am charging the Ord. Dept. of the Army, to whom I am told gives good satisfaction, there being no complaint or objection to the pistol.

I have sent you just what we are daily manufacturing. I can plate the guards and varnish the stocks if desired. The pistol is well balanced, efficient, durable, simple of construction, made of good materials and not liable to get out of order, all of which qualifications make it a very durable weapon. Waiting for a report from you concerning these pistols.

I remain,
Yours very respectfully
Eli Whitney [10]

The revolvers Whitney submitted to the Bureau were tested, and a favorable report was submitted on February 4, 1863, to Captain J.A. Dahlgren, Chief of Bureau of Ordnance.

In the letter, Naval Lieutenant Commander Skerett states he tested Whitney's revolver, "#17751, firing it 500 times before cleaning was required," and it "withstood the test admirably, and appears to be in as good condition as when received." After ten years of persistence, Eli Whitney had finally received a favorable report on his revolvers from the Navy. The Bureau immediately ordered 100 revolvers be sent to Cairo, Illinois, for the Navy, and 100 to the New York Navy Yard. In March 1863, another 100 Whitney Navy revolvers were requested for U.S. Ordnance Ship *Dale*, in Key West, Florida.

During the latter part of 1863, the Bureau began receiving unfavorable reports regarding Remington revolvers and the Johnson & Dow cartridges furnished with them. Between December 1863 and May 1864 the Bureau delayed ordering Remington revolvers. In January 1864, the inspector of ordnance at the New York Yard reported that due to "complaints of pistols issued to vessels, I directed my assistant Lt. Comdr. Young to test and carefully examine the last invoice of pistols received from Whitney and compare them to those received from Remington & Sons & herewith enclose his report." On January 9, 1864, a report regarding the examination and test firing of Whitney revolvers was submitted by Lt. Comdr. Young. The report covered the testing, by firing, of 100 Whitney revolvers using Whitney's cartridges. These cartridges were most likely manufactured by D.C. Sage Company of Middletown, Connecticut.[11] Only one failure was reported, "which was attributable to the nipple not having been drilled through." The report continued with praise for Whitney's revolvers:

"The range and penetration of these pistols were excellent, apparently greater than the Remington pistols with their best cartridge.

After firing, they were subjected to a careful examination of all their parts, and no defects were discovered. A pleasing uniformity in the construction of all the different parts of these pistols was observed. The cylinders were smoothly bored, the vent of the nipples were uniform and of proper size, the nipples when screwed in were well filled, and of uniform length, the cocks were tempered so that they could be filed, if necessary, and none were broken or defective; the main and sear springs were of uniform strength; the hand springs were of uniform length in no instance revolving the chamber beyond the clamp, or not far enough to permit the cock to strike fair on the cap.

A great want of uniformity in all their parts exists in the Remington revolvers, from a marked carelessness in their manufacture."[12]

There were two suggested improvements mentioned in the report.

"I can see only two objections to the Whitney pistols, which are easily remedied: The sight is too slender at the base making it more liable to be broken off by catching it in the holster, or receiving a light blow. By giving it a more conical shape would add to its strength. The second fault is in the rammer: The connecting link of the joint is rather slight, for rough handling, when too much force might be applied to push the ball home."[13]

Whitney was notified of this report and asked to consider the suggestions it contained. Orders for Whitney's revolvers resumed

Fig. 4: The initials of Frank C. Warner are stamped on the lower left side of the frame. *(Photo courtesy of Rock Island Auction Company)*

in February with the order of 300 revolvers. There was, however, one stipulation applied. Frank C. Warner, a civilian employee of the Washington Navy Yard, was to inspect all revolvers. Mr. Warner had been assigned to the Whitneyville Armory in May 1863 to inspect muskets.[14]

From this directive, we know that revolvers with the F.C.W. inspector's mark were procured beginning in February 1864. Revolvers in our survey that had this inspector's initials were 22514, 22603, 22739, 22774, 22782, 22788, 22795, 22868, 22888, 22991, 23079, 23434, and 23486.

Other revolvers listed in a study conducted by Ken Domina as having the F.C.W. inspector marking were serial numbers 22562, 22712, 22846, 22909, 22945, 23270, and 23383.

Warner's initials are found on the left frame below the space between the barrel and cylinder, as shown in Figure 4. Occasionally, a cartouche bearing the initials "*FCW*" may also be found on the upper portion of the left grip. The Warner markings are estimated to have begun somewhere around serial number 22500 and are found through approximately 24000. On May 16, 1864, Warner was directed to complete his duties at the Whitneyville Armory and return to Washington. There were 900 revolvers delivered during the time that Frank C. Warner was inspecting revolvers at Whitneyville.[15]

In a letter dated February 12, 1864, the Navy Ordnance Yard at Washington tested 42 Whitney revolvers. This letter is unique, in that the revolvers tested were listed by serial number. These revolvers were taken from a lot of 200 that were delivered around January 23, 1864, so they would not have been inspected by Warner.[16] The serial numbers of these revolvers were in the low 22000 and low 23000 ranges. The date of delivery, along with the serial numbers, helps determine the serial range of the Whitney revolvers delivered to the Navy.[17] See Appendix A for a list of these serial numbers.

It is evident in reviewing these numbers that Whitney did not deliver revolvers on a "first manufactured-first shipped" basis. As noted earlier, Warner was not inspecting revolvers when this batch was shipped; however, revolvers with his initials began appearing above the 22500 range.

Whitney continued to receive orders for his revolvers, which he was selling at $12 each. This was a lower cost than Remington was quoting (at $14, and later $13 each). In correspondence to Captain H.A. Wise, Chief of Ordnance dated June 4, 1864, Whitney informs Wise that he is shipping 250 revolvers as soon as possible. Whitney also references an inspection report that the Ordnance Bureau had sent to him:

"In reference to the report of Commodore Bell I would simply say that we will rectify the points he speaks of as soon as possible. The link on those now being made are thicker, and we have only 18 on hand of the thinner and they are of steel. The guard shall be made larger."[18]

This reference indicates that Whitney would begin producing revolvers with the larger trigger guards; however, this may not have occurred until 1865. The Navy ordered 100 revolvers on October 22, 1864, to be delivered to the Washington Ordnance Yard. These 100 revolvers were tested, and a report issued in a letter dated December 8, 1864, from the Navy Ordnance Yard, Washington City. Again serial numbers were listed, and these numbers are also provided in Appendix A. The rammer of one revolver (26318) broke "*while the pistol was being loaded owing to defectiveness of the metal.*"[19]

From this report it appears that Whitney was furnishing the Bureau with his entire revolver production. Approximately 3,450 revolvers were furnished between February and December 1864 (the period covered by these two reports). Whitney was producing about 350 revolvers per month during most of 1864.

These letters have helped to identify some of the improvements made in Whitney's revolvers, along with approximate dates of these changes. As mentioned before, the "Colt-style" lever catch is the feature that marked the transition to what we call the "3rd Type." This may have been one of the "improvements" requested by the Ordnance Bureau; however, it was certainly in use by mid-1862 when revolvers were shipped to the Army. We have seen the requests in January 1864 for a strengthened rammer and enhanced front sight, and in June 1864 for larger trigger guards, as well as the strengthening of the rammer. Whitney complied with these requests. The larger trigger guards were observed on revolvers beginning at approximately serial number 28000 and above; however, the author noted only one that was martially marked. It would have been among the last revolvers shipped to the Navy.

The last order for Whitney revolvers was sent on March 15, 1865:

Bureau of Ordnance
Navy Department
Washington March 15th, 1865

Mr. Eli Whitney
Whitneyville, Conn.
Sir:

Be pleased to forward as soon as possible, to the Navy Ordnance Yard in this City, marked "For the Potomac Flotilla":

(20) Twenty Navy Revolvers.

I am Sir, Your Obedient Servant
R. Aulick, Asst. Chief of Bureau [20]

Observations and Findings from the Whitney Survey

The earliest martially marked revolver in the author's study is serial number 1375, which is marked "U.S.N." on the butt strap. This revolver is illustrated in *U.S. Naval Handguns* by Fredrick R. Winter. Mr. Winter notes that this revolver has the iron trigger guard found on the First Model Whitney revolvers. While it may appear this is a First Model, 4th Type, the other characteristics indicate it is a Second Model, 1st Type. The revolver appears to have the stronger frame with a thicker top strap as well as a wing-nut, as seen on the Second Model. In addition it has the single safety slot, and the letters "BA" appear on the frame and under the trigger guard, both of which are indicative of an early Second Model. Regardless, this revolver is somewhat of a mystery, having the U.S.N. marking on the butt. Could this have been one of Whitney's early attempts to interest the Navy? Mr. Winter provided an excellent photograph of the butt marking in his book, and the author used that photograph to compare the marking with examples of U.S.N. markings provided in an article titled "Marking Variations of U.S. Naval Inspectors on Colt 1851 and 1861 Navy Model Revolvers Percussion and Conversion" by Sam Pachanian and L. Frank Richey.[21] The style of "U.S.N." marking used on the Whitney revolver appears to be consistent with those found on the Colt 1861 New Model Navy during 1861-62. This revolver also bears the "B" inspection marks on the barrel, cylinder, and trigger guard, as well as a cartouche on both grips. Mr. Winter notes that the cartouche markings are of inspectors serving during 1862. These markings indicate inspection for the Army. In Whitney's letter to Captain J.A. Dahlgren dated January 28, 1863, he shipped six revolvers to the Navy and stated "They are inspected in the regular way according to Army Regulations." (See letter in this Chapter.) These revolvers, and perhaps others, had the inspection markings required by the Army prior to being purchased by the Navy.

The next earliest martially marked revolver noted in the survey was serial number 1540. This Second Model revolver has inspector initials on the barrel, frame, cylinder, and trigger guard. Another early martially marked revolver observed by the author was serial number 6023. This revolver was marked with a "C" in various locations by an inspector and still had the "Ball-type" lever catch. Most of the martially marked revolvers began to appear above the 11000 serial range. The latest number we viewed was serial number 27739. One other revolver in the high 28000 range was reported as having Naval re-inspection initials on the cylinder. From this analysis, we determined that most of the martially marked revolvers were found in the 4th Type serial number range, with some scattered throughout the 3rd Type range. A few above the 28000 serial range also saw military service.

It was also determined that most of the martially marked revolvers purchased by the Army carried a "B" inspector's mark on the right side of the barrel and frame, left side of the barrel, on the cylinder, and on the bottom of the trigger guard. A cartouche is often found on the left grip.

Examples of martial markings for both the Army and Navy are provided in the following section of this chapter. Also included are examples of New Jersey marked revolvers, which were purchased in 1863 by that State. It should be remembered that the Army, as well as various states, purchased revolvers directly from private dealers early in the War. Many of those revolvers were not martially marked.

Inspection Marks found on U.S. Army Contract Revolvers:

Fig. 5: Inspector mark ("B") on right side of barrel and frame. *(Courtesy William Henry Lee collection)*

Fig. 6: Inspector mark on left side of barrel (and sometimes on frame). *(Courtesy William Henry Lee collection)*

Fig. 8: Trigger Guard: Inspector mark on brass trigger guard. *(Courtesy William Henry Lee collection)*

Fig. 7: Cylinder: Inspector mark can be seen on rear of cylinder, between the nipples. Often two letters will be found. *(Courtesy Hans Westberg)*

The Inspector's Cartouche is usually found only on the Left Grip

Fig. 9: The most often seen cartouche is "STB," Samuel Timothy Bugbee, as stamped on serial #14854. *(Courtesy Hans Westberg)*

Fig. 10: The cartouche of Pomeroy Booth, "PB," was noted on serial #23855. *(Author's collection)*

Fig. 11: Three Union cavalry soldiers showing off their revolvers. The soldier on the right holds a Whitney revolver. *(Courtesy Medhurst & Co.)*

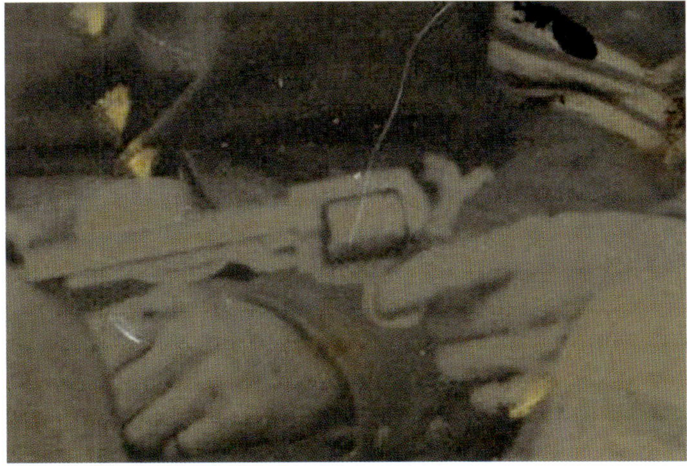

Fig. 12: Close up of the Whitney Navy revolver. *(Courtesy Medhurst & Co.)*

Union cavalryman armed with a Whitney Navy revolver. *(Courtesy Matthew Fleming, The Civil War Image Shop)*

The following chart indicates the number of Whitney Navy revolvers purchased by the Army. Approximately 28% of those purchases were from private vendors.

Army Purchases of Whitney Revolvers

Source	1861	1862	1863	1864
Dickson & Gilmore	10			
M. Felsenthal	21			
Phillip S. Justice	400	797		
State of New Jersey			170	622
Palmer & Batchelders	310			
A.B. Semple & Sons			87	
Schuyler, Hartley & Graham	540		14	
Ira D. Thompson		14		
Eli Whitney		5601	2001	
Total per Year	**1281**	**6412**	**2272**	**622**

There were seven private vendors from which the U.S. Army purchased Whitney revolvers. Contracts with the Whitney Armory began in March 1862 and ended with the last purchase in February 1863. There were 792 Whitney revolvers obtained from the State of New Jersey in 1863 and 1864.

The above purchases indicate a total of 10,587 Whitney Navy revolvers procured by the U.S. Army. (The author noted another 597 "Navy Revolvers" procured by the U.S. Army from Phillip S. Justice in 1861. These may have been Whitney revolvers, but were not noted as such in Ordnance Department Records.)

State of New Jersey

The state of New Jersey purchased about 920 Whitney revolvers in 1863. The U.S. Army purchased 792 of these revolvers from New Jersey in 1863-64.[22] The two revolvers shown below demonstrate the markings of that state.

Whitney Navy Revolver #15001 (New Jersey marked) with Holster

This revolver is stamped "NJ" on the left side of the barrel near the frame and on the left frame below the cylinder (see photograph below).

Fig. 13: "NJ" stamped on the left side of barrel and on frame. *(Courtesy of Richard MacDonald)*

The holster, shown here, was manufactured by J. Davy Company, Newark, NJ.

Fig. 15: *(Courtesy of Richard MacDonald)*

Fig. 14: *(Courtesy of Richard MacDonald)*

Fig. 16: "N.J." stamped on the left side of the barrel. *(Photo courtesy of James D. Julia Auctioneers)*

There were seven revolvers noted in the survey that were identified as "New Jersey" revolvers. These were found in the 10000, 11000, 12000, 15000, and 16000 serial number ranges.

Some revolvers have "N.J." stamped on the barrel only, such as this one in the 11000 range, shown at left.

Donald L. Ware, author of *Remington Army and Navy Revolvers 1861-1888*, also noted both types of New Jersey markings on Remington revolvers. Mr. Ware indicated there were two sets of dies used: "Revolvers stamped with a 1/16-inch die are usually marked in two locations, on the left side of the frame below the cylinder and on the left barrel flat. The larger 1/8-inch die stamps were applied only to the left barrel flat."[23]

The Whitney revolvers shown in the above photographs are consistent with his findings.

Inspection Marks found on U.S. Navy Contract Revolvers

The U.S. Navy had no formal inspection markings during the first part of the War. Some Colt 1851 and 1861 Navy Models were stamped with "USN" and inspectors' initials on the butt as final acceptance markings, and some were not. Very few of the Whitney revolvers in this study had "USN" stamped on the butt. The one mentioned above (serial #1375) and serial numbers 23270 and 25715 were noted as having the "USN" marking.

Fig. 17: Serial #25715 was stamped "USN." *(Photo courtesy of James D. Julia Auctioneers)*

In August 1864, the following directive for the inspection of arms was issued by the Chief of the Bureau of Ordnance, Captain Henry A. Wise:

BUREAU OF ORDNANCE
NAVY DEPARTMENT
WASHINGTON CITY, Aug. 29, 1864

This Bureau directs that hereafter all small arms, when passed by the inspector, be stamped in the following manner:

MUSKETS, CARBINES, and PISTOLS.

*On top of the barrel near the breech, with an anchor; and, on the lock-plate, the letter **P** over the initials of the Inspector, thus: **P / A.B.***

REVOLVERS

*On top of the barrel, near the cylinder, with an anchor, and on the face of the cylinder, the letter **P** over the initials of the inspector, as above.*

CUTLASSES.

*On the blade, immediately below the guard, with an anchor, and the letter **P** over the initials of the Inspector, as above.*

The Bureau will furnish to each Inspector two sizes of stamps. MUSKET CARBINES and CUTLASSES are to be marked with the larker, (.15-in.,) and PISTOLS and REVOLVERS with the smaller (.1-in.,) size of stamps.

H.A. WISE,
Chief of Bureau[23]

Fig. 18: Anchor stamp. *(Courtesy of Ed Kushner)*

Fig. 19: Inspector's initials. *(Courtesy of Ed Kushner)*

The initials "WNJ" shown in Figure 19 are those of Lieutenant Commander William N. Jeffers, Washington Navy Yard.

Naval Inspectors for other Navy Yards also stamped their initials on revolvers that passed inspection. See Figure 20 below.

The "P," along with the inspector's initials, is often seen on the side of the cylinder, as shown below. Occasionally a "U.S." is also found stamped on the top of the barrel (an example may be seen in Chapter Eight). These markings are believed to be from the "re-inspection" conducted at the conclusion of the Civil War. The Navy reexamined their weapons to determine those suitable for retention in the Navy's inventory. Weapons that had been unmarked prior to the 1864 directive were also marked if retained in inventory.

Fig. 20: Inspector's initials. *(Courtesy of Marc Williams)*

Fig. 21: *(Photo courtesy of James D. Julia Auctioneers)*

Five-Groove Barrel Rifling

Five-groove barrel rifling was first noted in the martially marked Navy revolvers. However, the seven-groove rifling appeared to be the standard in most of the martially marked revolvers examined by the author. Whether Whitney was experimenting with the use of five-groove rifling, or perhaps using that process to save time as he filled Naval contracts, is unknown. Two examples of the five-groove rifling are shown below:

This U.S. Navy revolver has inspector initials properly placed on the face of the cylinder (see Figure 20 above). These initials appear to be "CC," with one initial facing downward. An anchor appears on the barrel. This revolver was the earliest one noted with five-groove rifling.

Fig. 22: Whitney Navy Revolver #25127. *(Courtesy of Marc Williams)*

Fig. 23: Five-groove rifling. *(Courtesy of Marc Williams)*

Fig. 24: Anchor stamp on barrel of #25127. *(Courtesy of Marc Williams)*

Fig. 25: Whitney Navy revolver #26222. *(Courtesy of Ed Kushner)*

The revolver in Figure 25 is on the list of revolvers inspected by the Navy on December 8, 1864, at the Washington Navy Yard (see Appendix A). This revolver has a barrel that is six and one half inches in length. The opinion of the author is that the barrel would have been shortened following the revolver's service in the Navy. The initials of Lieutenant Commander William N. Jeffers appear on the face of the cylinder, and an anchor is stamped on the barrel.

This revolver also has the five-groove barrel rifling. Perhaps Whitney made the change from seven grooves to five grooves as he rushed to meet the deadlines of his Navy contracts.

Fig. 26: *(Courtesy of Ed Kushner)*

Fig. 27: *(Courtesy of Ed Kushner)*

The following chart indicates the number of Whitney Navy revolvers purchased by the Navy.

Navy Purchases of Whitney Revolvers

Destination	1863	1864	1865
Cairo, IL	250		
New York Navy Yard	820	1800	
Baltimore, MD	20		
St. Louis, MO	26		
Ft. Monroe, VA	100		
Portsmouth, NH Navy Yard	190	200	
Boston Navy Yard	750	400	
Washington Navy Yard	350	100	120
Mound City, IL		300	
Philadelphia Navy Yard		700	100
Total per Year	**2506**	**3500**	**220**

The Navy purchased 6,226 Whitney Navy Revolvers from February 4, 1863, through March 15, 1865. A detailed listing of revolver purchases by the Navy is provided on the following page.

The serial numbers for these revolvers began as early as 17751 (which was one of the six revolvers Whitney sent for inspection in January 1863). Many of the revolvers delivered prior to August 1864 had no inspection markings, but were later inventoried and stamped with an anchor on the barrel after the War. Based on the author's survey, the majority of the Navy marked revolvers were found in the 19000-27800 serial number range.

The contracts that Whitney procured with the Army and Navy during the Civil War helped to secure a place in history for his revolvers. Of all the revolvers produced by Eli Whitney, the most easily recognized and the most often seen is his Navy Revolver.

WHITNEY REVOLVERS ORDERED BY BUREAU OF ORDNANCE, U.S. NAVY 1863-1865

DATE OF ORDER	DATE SHIPPED*	DELIVERED TO	TOTAL	PRICE PAID	
2/ 4/63	2/21/63	Cairo, Illinois, Mississippi Squadron	100	$12	00
2/ 4/63	3/21/63	N.Y. Navy Yard, Western Gulf Squadron	100	$12	00
3/ 4/63	3/17/63	Fortress Monroe, Virginia	100	$12	00
3/14/63	3/28/63	Baltimore Naval Station	20	$12	00
3/17/63	3/21/63	St. Louis, Mo., Mississippi Squadron	26	$12	00
3/18/63	3/27/63	N.Y. Navy Yard, Ord. Store Ship "Dale"	100	$12	00
3/31/63	4/ 4/63	N.Y. Navy Yard, S. Atlantic Blockade Sq.	30	$12	00
4/23/63	5/ 1/63	Portsmouth N.H. Navy Yard	150	$12	00
5/18/63	5/25/63	Cairo, Illinois, Mississippi Squadron	150	$12	00
5/22/63	5/27/63	Portsmouth N.H. Navy Yard	40	$12	00
6/29/63	7/10/63	Boston Navy Yard	300	$12	00
6/29/63	8/12/63	Boston Navy Yard	450	$12	00
8/14/63	8/25/63	Washington Ordnance Yard, U.S.S. Eutaw	100	$12	00
9/14/63	10/ 2/63	N.Y.Navy Yard	250	$12	00
9/15/63	9/24/63	Washington Ordnance Yard, "Roanoke"	50	$12	00
9/21/63	10/10/63	N.Y. Navy Yard, "Sloop Dale"	100	$12	00
9/26/63	10/14/63	N.Y. Navy Yard, for Mare Island, Ca.	40	$12	00
10/ 5/63	1/23/64	Washington Ordnance Yard	200	$12	00
10/ 5/63	12/31/63	N.Y. Navy Yard, for "New Orleans"	100	$12	00
11/13/63	1/28/64	N.Y. Navy Yard, for California	100	$12	00
2/ 1/64	2/16/64	Mound City, Illinois, Miss. Squadron	300	$12	00
2/ 8/64	3/ 4/64	New York Navy Yard	200	$12	00
2/22/64	3/16/64	Philadelphia Navy Yard	200	$12	00
4/20/64	4/23/64	New York Navy Yard	200	$12	00
5/18/64	6/ 8/64	Boston Navy Yard	100	$12	00
5/18/64	7/ 5/64	New York Navy Yard	400	$12	00
6/ 2/64	7/ 6/64	New York Navy Yard	50	$12	00
6/ 2/64	7/16/64	New York Navy Yard	50	$12	00
6/ 2/64	8/31/64	New York Navy Yard	50	$12	00
6/ 2/64	9/14/64	New York Navy Yard	100	$12	00
6/ 8/64	9/16/64	New York Navy Yard	100	$12	00
6/ 8/64	9/22/64	New York Navy Yard	100	$12	00
6/ 8/64	9/24/64	New York Navy Yard	100	$12	00
6/ 8/64	10/ 1/64	New York Navy Yard	50	$12	00
6/ 8/64	10/17/64	New York Navy Yard	50	$12	00
6/ 8/64	10/18/64	New York Navy Yard	50	$12	00
6/ 8/64	1/21/65	New York Navy Yard	50	$12	00
8/15/64	9/ 5/64	Philadelphia Navy Yard	100	$14	00
8/15/64	9/ 8/64	Philadelphia Navy Yard	100	$14	00
8/15/64	9/12/64	Philadelphia Navy Yard	100	$14	00
9/ 2/64	1/21/65	Portsmouth N.H.	200	$14	00
10/ 3/64	1/21/65	Boston Navy Yard	300	$14	00
10/22/64	11/ 6/64	Washington Ordnance Yard	100	$14	00
10/24/64	11/15/64	Philadelphia Navy Yard	100	$14	00
10/24/64	11/19/64	Philadelphia Navy Yard	100	$14	00
12/15/64	3/ 1/65	N.Y. Navy Yard, For Mound City Illinois	250	$14	00
2/27/65	3/ 1/65	Philadelphia Navy Yard	100	$14	00
3/ 6/65	3/13/65	Washington Ord. Yard, for Norfolk Va.	100	$14	00
3/15/65	4/18/65	Washington Ord. Yard, Potomac Flotilla	20	$14	00
		Total	6,226		

* Some of these dates may not be the actual dates of delivery; they are however, the dates entered into the Bureau Records.

Fig. 28: *(Courtesy Don Ware and Ken Domina Research Records)*

Private William Gardner, Co. B, 1st NC Artillery, holds a Whitney Navy revolver. (*Courtesy of Greensboro Historical Museum Archives*)

6

WHITNEYS FOR THE SOUTH

During the late 1850s and into 1860 tensions built between the southern states and the federal government. States throughout the South began arming their militias by any means possible. Whitney Firearms Company was one of many sources used. In his book *Civil War Pistols*, John D. McAulay states that Maryland purchased 1,000 Whitney revolvers, and Virginia also purchased some Whitneys that were used by their Cavalry.[1]

In the author's research, the following letters were located in the online archives of the Virginia Military Institute. This correspondence occurs following the raid on Harper's Ferry in 1859. The State of Virginia had determined that it needed to improve the arms of its militia, and legislation to this effect was passed in the Virginia General Assembly in 1860, with funds appropriated for the private purchase of arms. To oversee this effort, the Virginia Armory Commission was created. Three men were appointed to the Commission: Col. Philip St. George Cocke, Maj. George W. Randolph, and Col. Francis H. Smith. Col. Francis H. Smith served as Superintendent of the Virginia Military Institute from 1839-1889. The following letters are some of Smith's correspondence in which he mentions the purchase of Whitney's revolvers. Adams, who is referred to in some of the letters, is Soloman Adams, Master Armorer of the Virginia Armory in 1860, and later of the Confederate Ordnance. Some wording is illegible, but the author felt the references to Whitney revolvers would be of interest to collectors. Those references are highlighted in bold.[2]

Va Military Institute
Oct 31 1860
Capt Geo W. Randolph
Richmond Va
My dear Sir,

I have yours of the 29' this morning. Adams has been with me since yesterday, and after a full conference with Maj. Colston in reference to the model musket we have finally concluded upon the changes allowable in the U.S. Model. They are not internal and will not affect the length of the barrel or bayonet. I have said to him that I would be in favor of **getting 500 of Whitney's pistol if he would attach a pin as to keep the hammer from falling upon the cap thus securing the safeguard (unclear, unclear).** Adams thinks that Whitney [unclear] do this. The price of $12. Adams to inspect them all before use. I [would?] by all means have all the pistols from Ames examined by Adams [... *The remainder of the page is unreadable. Next page*: ...] Cavalry equipments which Col. Cocke gets [...]. I agree with you that it is right and proper [unclear] and the Law imposes it as a duty upon us. We must consider however that every thousand dollars saved will enable us to do more towards arming and supplying the state. If it be found advisable to employ an ordnance man to make the fuses [unclear?] you had better let my [unclear] Sergeant take the matter in hand. He is a first rate man & will do it well. I will send you [unclear] 4 sets of harness – that is – for 8 horses, by express – via Staunton. Deduct the $1.75 I owe you from my accounts when you [unclear] and send the harness down to Adams. I hope Anderson will employ Burton* & that he may also secure his services. /FHS/

V. M. Institute
Nov. 6 1860
Gen W. H. Richardson
Richmond

My dear Sir,

I have yours of the 4'. If Dimmock needs a temporary clerk I would cheerfully assent to his employing one if Capt Randolph concurs. I like the D & A [*Deane and Adams*] pistol better than Colts'. It is more handy and more manageable. Some of the nipples are defective. We paid too much for them – but that was a part of our Contract for (unclear). **I think I would get 500 of Whitney Pistol at (H.A.?) a good (arm?).** We have some reports of (trouble?) in Amherst. I don't heed them, except to be on the (unclear). /FHS/ - - - - - - - - - - - - - -

Va Military Institute
Nov 20 1860
Richmond Va
Capt G W Randolph
Richmond Va

My dear Sir,

I have a letter from Gen. Richardson this morning about the Harnesses. If I was not explicit enough (unclear) a reference to them, I must be now, for his sake, as he had

great trouble in getting them for the cadets & I must not be so ungracious even to equip your good company, as to show a want of appreciation of his kind offer. I mean, you must return an equivalent set when they are [unclear] & as this may not be in your power, when we are [unclear] hope you had better have a set made now by [unclear]. My idea originally was to save the (Express?) but I reckon your Company will want them always & ought to have them. I have no doubt your Company is going to be one of the most efficient in the state. I notice the article in the Dispatch [*Richmond newspaper*] this morning which I presume is [unclear]. It is very well. I send you the enclosed advertisement. If you think it worth while send it to Van Nostrand and authorize them to buy the muskets if he can get them at a price not exceeding $2.50. It may be worth while. But I have it [unclear]. **Adams writes that Whitney has made the modifications in the Pistol, which makes it a superior weapon. I would certainly take 500 of them at $12 & if you agree, let Adams know.** Don't forget about the Report. Let it be full & in detail & present clearly the financial view. /FHS/
- - - - - - - -

Va Military Institute
Nov 30 1860
Capt Geo W. Randolph
Richmond Va

My dear Sir,

I have yours of the 28' this morning, and will prepare the White Sulphur Report in a few days. I am glad you have closed engagements for the Caps, balls etc and would not be surprized if it may no be necessary for you to double this order. I have no percussion caps here at all & I feel very much the want of them & must beg of you to send me a supply as soon as they are in hand. **Whitney seems to be very anxious to sell us his pistol. I have sent to him a reply, that if he will estimate our bonds at 92 & charge no exchange on Va Money, we might (take?) 500 of them at $12. My expectation is he will accept & if so I would by all means take them. It is a very fine pistol.** The powder is rec'd & I have it stored away in our new Magazine which was completed the day it arrived. I have rec'd no invoice of the quantity sent, but have received some 254 Barrels. I have a letter from Col Cocke today dated New Orleans Nov 24. He says the 8 cotton States will certainly go out & Va should be prepared to act with them. The sentiment here is much short of my own feeling in this Crisis & unless the [unclear] additional Constitutional guarantees are given us, we have no alternative than to go out also. You were fortunate in the Contract for accoutrements. /FHS/

[Note: *On 20 December, a state convention in South Carolina voted an ordinance declaring the immediate secession of the state from the Union.*]

Va Military Institute
Dec 20 1860
Capt Geo W. Randolph
Richmond Va

My dear Sir,

I have yours of the 18' this morning and I hasten to reply to it by return mail. I had certainly understood that the barrel rolling machine was embraced in the estimate, and that the price charged by Ames was the consideration that induced (Sheet? Steel?) firm in New York to make a friendly hint to us on the subject. This led to an explanation with Mr. Ames, the result of which was satisfactory to the Commissioners. Could I be mistaken in this? If I am, & it should clearly appear that Anderson's contract does not embrace it, we shall have to get it upon the best terms we may. Do the best you can – I will stand up to your action. I would by all means get the 500 pistols & the 400 rifles, if the Colts are warranted but not otherwise. **Dr. Graham of Lexington has been acting as a sort of Agent for Whitney, & when I suggested to him that Whitney might sell his pistols to us at $12, if he would take our stock at $90 & knock off Exchange, I thought he was inclined to accept. You will find a readiness on the part of Whitney to make some compromise in this way.** Do the best you can. I send you a letter of Ames. I have omitted such parts of it as do not come under the head of the usual implements supplied to the School by the state. We are actually reduced to nothing & could not have paraded the cadets so destitute were we of them.
/FHS/ - - - - -

These letters indicate that the state of Virginia would have purchased at least 500 Whitney revolvers in early 1861. The "modifications" that Col Smith refers to were probably the addition of the safety notch, or notches to the revolver's cylinder. His wording of "*if he would attach a pin as to keep the hammer from falling upon the cap*" is probably a reference to the safety pins used on Colt's firearms to keep the hammer from touching the percussion cap when the hammer is lowered. Rather than using Colt's "safety pin" concept, Whitney used a "safety notch" on the back of the cylinder, between the nipples. We could speculate that it was the addition of a single safety slot, or notch, as found on the Second Model, 1st Type revolver. One of these Whitney revolvers was selected as a pattern for the Confederacy's Spiller & Burr. The fact that the early Spiller & Burr revolvers had a single safety notch as well as the ball-type lever latch and a wing-nut would indicate the model used as a pattern was the Second Model, 1st Type

Whitney.[3] However, the author did locate several Second Model, 2nd Type revolvers that were associated with Confederate officers. These revolvers have been identified as "Virginia-used," but it is unknown when the officers acquired them. They could have been privately purchased prior to succession or captured during the War, or possibly among those purchased by the state of Virginia. Those revolvers include the following serial numbers:

#2796 used by Bishop Alfred Magill Randolph, a Virginian who served as a Confederate Army chaplain. (Museum of the Confederacy)

#2814 used by Commodore William F. Lynch, CSN, a Virginian who resigned from the U.S. Navy to serve with his state. He first served as a Captain in the Virginia Navy and then in the Confederate States Navy. (Museum of the Confederacy)

#3110 used by General JEB Stuart, a Virginian who commanded the First Virginia Cavalry early in the war, and later commanded the Confederate Cavalry Corp of the Army of Northern Virginia. (Virginia Historical Society) (See Figure 1)

Another Whitney Navy revolver in the collection of the Virginia Historical Society is serial number 1599. It is inscribed

Fig. 1: Revolver of JEB Stuart, serial number 3110. This revolver was used by Stuart when mortally wounded at the Battle of Yellow Tavern, May 11, 1864. *(Courtesy of the Virginia Historical Society)*

Fig. 2: James Ewell Brown (JEB) Stuart (February 6, 1833 – May 12, 1864). *(Courtesy of the Library of Congress)*

on the trigger guard "*Lt Col Samuel T. Harison*"; however, there is no record of this individual serving in the Confederate Army. Perhaps he served in an early militia unit.

Whitney Navy revolver serial number 2255 has a Kentucky Confederate connection. "*J.S.G. Gay, Winchester Ky*" is etched on this revolver. Research indicates this was Jonathan Stamper Gardner Gay, a Captain in the 8th Kentucky Cavalry, CSA, serving under General John Hunt Morgan. Gay was taken prisoner during Morgan's raid into Ohio and held as prisoner for two years at Johnson's Island, Ohio.

Another Whitney Navy revolver, serial number 3826, is inscribed to Confederate Colonel Charles C. Lee, 37th NC Troops. This documented revolver was sold in 2005 by Greg Martin Auctions.

Other Whitney Navy revolvers with Confederate connections include serial numbers 6834 and 10295. Serial number 6834 has a verbal provenance of being owned by James W. Sinclair, 43rd Battalion Virginia Cavalry, Mosby's Command. Serial number 10295 is inscribed to an officer of the 13th Mississippi Volunteers. These revolvers are listed in Appendix C.

Any sale of revolvers to a southern state by the Whitney Arms Company occurred prior to the succession of that state, and most likely would have been low serial numbers of the Second Model, 2nd Type, as well as those of the 1st Type. Perhaps some First Models were sold to the South as well. Whitney revolvers may have also been purchased from any of the numerous private firms, just as the U.S. Ordnance Department did prior to its contracts with Eli Whitney. The heaviest concentration of martially marked revolvers, which the U.S. Government purchased directly from Whitney, began to appear in the 13000 to 27000 range, although a few are found scattered below that range.

There are also several photographs in existence of Confederate soldiers with Whitney revolvers. The photograph in Figure 5 is of a Confederate soldier holding a Whitney revolver, and appears to have been made early in the War. This photograph is of Micajah Van Landingham, who served in the Warren Guards, a volunteer militia company from Warren County, North Carolina. Van Landingham later served in Company C, 46th Regiment N.C. State Troops and surrendered at Appomattox on April 9, 1865.

Fig. 3: Revolver of Captain J.S.G. Gay, 8th Kentucky Cavalry, CSA. Serial number 2255. (*Courtesy of James A. Rogers, Sr.*)

Fig. 3a: *J.S.G. GAY, WINCHESTER KY* is etched on the right barrel flat of this revolver. (*Courtesy of James A. Rogers, Sr.*)

Fig. 4: Revolver of Colonel Charles C. Lee, 37th NC troops, serial number 3826. *(Courtesy of Greg Martin Auctions)*

Fig. 4a: Inside gripstrap marked 37. Butt inscribed N.C.T. [North Carolina Troops]. Backstrap inscribed Col. Charles C. Lee. Jig-bone carved walnut grips. *(Courtesy of Greg Martin Auctions)*

Many of the weapons used by the Confederacy were arms captured in battle. The Whitney revolvers were certainly among those captured and put to use by the South.

While conducting research for this book, the author found that a number of these revolvers were documented to have been carried by the 4th Virginia "Blackhorse" Cavalry. Mr. Tim Prince, of College Hill Arsenal, provided the author more detailed information regarding these revolvers:

"A list of 24 Whitney revolvers exists that link some revolvers in the mid-11000 serial number range; the upper-mid 14000 and lower 15000 ranges; and the upper 17000 to low 18000 range to this famous cavalry unit. The list is a period document cataloging by serial number the Whitney Navy revolvers that were being repaired for the 4th VA. The owner of the document wishes to remain anonymous and is not willing to release the list of serial numbers at this time. Martially marked Whitney revolvers are found in all of these serial number ranges, indicating the possibility of their capture from Union forces. However, the guns may also have been purchased on the open market by Southern agents working clandestinely. After comparing the 4th VA serial list against the Whitney Navy serial numbers documented in "Springfield Research Service Serial Numbers of US Martial Arms – Volume 4", one of the 4th VA guns (in the 18XXX range) was discovered to be only 2 numbers lower than a gun listed as being in the possession of Company D of the 21st PA Cavalry in 1864. No guns on the S.R.S. list were found on the 4th VA list, although several guns were found to be within 10 numbers of each other on the two lists. This supports the theory that at least some of the 4th VA guns were captured in the field."[4]

The following revolver, which resides in the Eli Whitney Museum, may well have been a captured revolver that was damaged and repaired using parts and techniques available in the Confederacy. Serial number 15235 is a martially marked revolver, bearing a cartouche on the left grip. An early barrel, serial number 1378, was used to replace the original barrel of this revolver. There is no visible barrel address. The lever appears to have been an

Fig. 6: Close-up of Van Landingham's Whitney Revolver. *(Courtesy of Thomas R. Van Landingham, great grandson of Micajah Van Landingham)*

Fig. 5: Micajah Van Landingham served in the Warren Guards, a North Carolina militia unit. *(Courtesy of Thomas R. Van Landingham, great grandson of Micajah Van Landingham)*

Fig. 7: Serial number 15235. Modified "ball-type" lever latch to accept the "Colt-style" lever. *(Courtesy of the Eli Whitney Museum)*

unnumbered Colt (or similar style) loading lever that was adapted to the Whitney cylinder pin. The barrel has a "ball-type" lever latch which has been modified to accept the "Colt-style" lever.

This revolver has no wing-nut, nor does it have any visible hole for a wing-nut or screw of any type.

The Texas Confederates in Figures 10 and 11 (following pages) both hold Whitney revolvers. The soldier in Figure 11 holds a Whitney and possibly a Colt Navy revolver, along with a D-Guard Bowie knife. Both revolvers have blade sights.

Fig. 8: Serial number 15235. Right side. *(Courtesy of the Eli Whitney Museum)*

Fig. 9: Serial number 15235. Left side. *(Courtesy of the Eli Whitney Museum)*

Fig. 10: Private John S. Pickle, Company B, 18th Texas cavalry. *(Austin History Center, Austin Public Library)*

Fig. 11: Matthew Wallace Hall, Corporal, Company K, 36th Texas cavalry (Woods' regiment) – also known as the 32nd Texas cavalry. *(Courtesy of Delpha Weatherson)*

The revolvers of Eli Whitney, Jr., would influence firearms of the Confederacy, as well as other firearms of the United States

7

WHITNEY'S INFLUENCE ON CONFEDERATE REVOLVERS AND OTHER WHITNEY COPIES

In addition to the South's early purchases of arms from Northern manufacturers, and along with the import of weapons from Europe, the Confederate states also turned to the manufacture of their own weapons. This chapter will briefly discuss two firms in the Confederate States that based their revolvers on the design of Eli Whitney. First we will examine the influence of Whitney's Navy Revolver on the revolvers of Spiller and Burr, and then those revolvers manufactured by T.W. Cofer.

Spiller and Burr

The phrase "Imitation is the sincerest form of flattery" could be used to describe the admiration that the South had for some of the Northern firearms manufacturers. The firearms of Colt (especially the Colt Model 1851 Navy) were the most often copied, but they were also the most plentiful, and had been in use since the early 1850s. The Whitney Navy revolver soon joined this special group of firearms that the South chose to copy.

Established by Lt. Col. James H. Burton, CSA, at the request of the Confederate Chief of Ordnance, the private manufacturing firm Spiller & Burr was to manufacture revolvers for the Confederate cavalry. Burton had a wealth of experience in the manufacture of small arms, as well as knowledge of the machinery required for such operations. He had acquired this experience in the United States and England during the years prior to the Civil War. When Virginia seceeded, Burton returned to assist his State to prepare for war. He was commissioned a lieutenant colonel in Virginia's Ordnance Department, in charge of the Virginia State Armory.[1]

The firm Spiller & Burr began in Richmond, Virginia, through the efforts of Edward N. Spiller and David J. Burr. Burton secured contracts for Spiller & Burr and acted as a chief engineer, ensuring the necessary mechanical arrangements of the firm. In late 1861, a contract between Spiller & Burr and the Confederate States of America provided that their firm would be paid between $25 and $30 (1861 CSA dollars) per revolver.[2] The contract further specified a revolver similar to a .36 caliber Navy revolver, Colt's model. Colt's Navy revolver had been adopted by the Confederate government as a standard revolver, but Lt. Col. Burton felt another type of revolver was superior to Colt's. Burton chose the Whitney as the pattern due to its performance, stability, design, and ease of construction. Since the State of Virginia had purchased Whitney Navy revolvers in 1860, Burton could easily have had access to one or more of these revolvers.[3] Thus, Spiller & Burr's revolver would become the "Southern Whitney" (see Figures 1, 2, and 3).

In 1862, with the Union Army approaching Richmond during the Peninsula Campaign, the pistol factory of Spiller & Burr moved to Atlanta, Georgia. Burton also traveled to Georgia to establish a permanent national armory, which was established in Macon, Georgia. The earliest Spiller & Burr revolvers were similar to the Second Model 1st Type Whitney Navy revolver, having the "ball-type" loading lever and catch, a single safety notch, and wing-nut. It had an open space between the face of the cylinder and the forepart of the frame. The barrel was screwed into the frame and passed through, so that the threads are visible just as they are on the Whitney Navy revolver. It differed from the Whitney in that its frame was brass and the cylinder was iron.

The first revolvers were inspected by Major W.S. Downer, Superintendent of the Richmond Armoury, in December 1862. Twelve revolvers were delivered and inspected, and Downer found "no defects in them."[4]

There are very few surviving revolvers of the first model Spiller & Burr. One of these rare first models is pictured in Figure 1.

In the spring of 1863, 40 revolvers were finished and delivered to the Macon Armoury. Unfortunately, 33 of those revolvers were rejected after testing and sent back to Spiller & Burr. These revolvers had major defects, such as the chambers not being in line with the bore of the barrel. The seven remaining revolvers were accepted. These revolvers had incorporated the following changes recommended by Downer:

- *The ball catch system to the loading lever was discontinued and replaced by a spring and catch similar to that of the Colt*
- *Six safety notches were cut in the shields between the nipples, where the head of the hammer could fit in to block the cylinder*

The recommendations for the Colt-style lever and catch and the addition of safety notches on the cylinder were the same changes that Eli Whitney had made in his revolver.[5]

One problem that plagued all arms manufacturers in the South was the lack of manufacturing material, such as steel. Spiller & Burr was fortunate to be the only Confederate revolver with steel barrels; however, cylinders were made of twisted iron, which provided some additional strength. Failure of the cylinders, along with the use of brass in the frames, often resulted in top straps being bulged due to the heavy explosion of powder in the chambers. That failure prompted Spiller & Burr to find a way to strengthen the frames of their revolvers, and this led to the production of the second model.[6]

The Second Model Spiller & Burr had a reinforced frame, so that the barrel threads were no longer visible. The thicker brass frame filled the open area that existed on the first model: see Figures 2 and 3.

The Confederate Government had contracted with Spiller & Burr for 15,000 revolvers; however, only about 1,450 were produced by the time the war ended. Between 1862 and January 1864, Spiller & Burr produced approximately 750 revolvers in Atlanta. In January 1864, the firm was purchased by the Confederate government and relocated to Macon, Georgia. Approximately 700 more revolvers were produced at that location.[7]

Fig. 1: Open framed First Model Spiller & Burr revolver. Marked "SPILLER & BURR" on top of barrel. Barrel serial No. 79, arbor pin serial No. 17, and loading lever serial No. 6. Revolver has the distinctive twist lines in the cylinder. This is one of only three Confederate First Model "Open Frame" Spiller & Burr Revolvers known to be extent with the rear threaded section of barrel exposed and with the thin top strap, having faithfully copied the Whitney revolver. Only seven of these revolvers passed inspection, of the first forty revolvers presented for inspection in May 1863. *(Courtesy of The Hayes Otoupalik Collection. Photo by: Darin Deyo)*

Fig. 2: Standard conventional 2nd Model Spiller & Burr revolver. Barrel marked "SPILLER & BURR" and serial No. 214. This has the Brass frame, which comes flush with the front of the cylinder to reinforce the end of the barrel and the thick top strap. The back strap is engraved "Luke to John." The Spiller & Burr was redesigned to correct the problems encountered with the first model design, and these conventional 2nd Models were the type manufactured through the end of production and assembly at Macon, Georgia. *(Courtesy of The Hayes Otoupalik Collection. Photo by: Darin Deyo)*

Fig. 3: Another Spiller & Burr standard model revolver, serial number 345. "CS" stamped on left side of frame. *(Photo courtesy of James D. Julia Auctioneers)*

T.W. Cofer

The Cofer revolvers were produced by Thomas W. Cofer, a gunmaker in Portsmouth, Virginia. In August 1861, the Confederate Patent Office granted patent number nine to Cofer for the production of a revolver that could use both the conventional percussion system and a metallic cartridge.

Cofer's revolver is partially based on the Whitney Navy revolver pattern, except for the spur trigger. The earlier Cofer revolvers lacked a loading lever, and were similar to the First Model, 1st Type Whitney revolvers. It is a .36 caliber, six shot revolver with a brass frame and a blued steel barrel and cylinder. The barrel is octagonal and 7 1/2 inches in length: see Figures 4 and 5.

The marking on the topstrap is "T.W. COFER'S / PATENT", and the address "PORTSMOUTH, VA" appears on top of the barrel. Those markings were stamped with individual die stamps for each letter. It is estimated that perhaps 86 to 140 were produced, while only about a dozen are known to exist today. The Cofer revolvers appear to have assembly markings but no serial numbers. Recent research of Confederate archives indicate that Cofer received at least one order from the Confederate government for 82 revolvers. All of those revolvers were issued to the 5th Virginia Cavalry Regiment sometime around May 1862.[8]

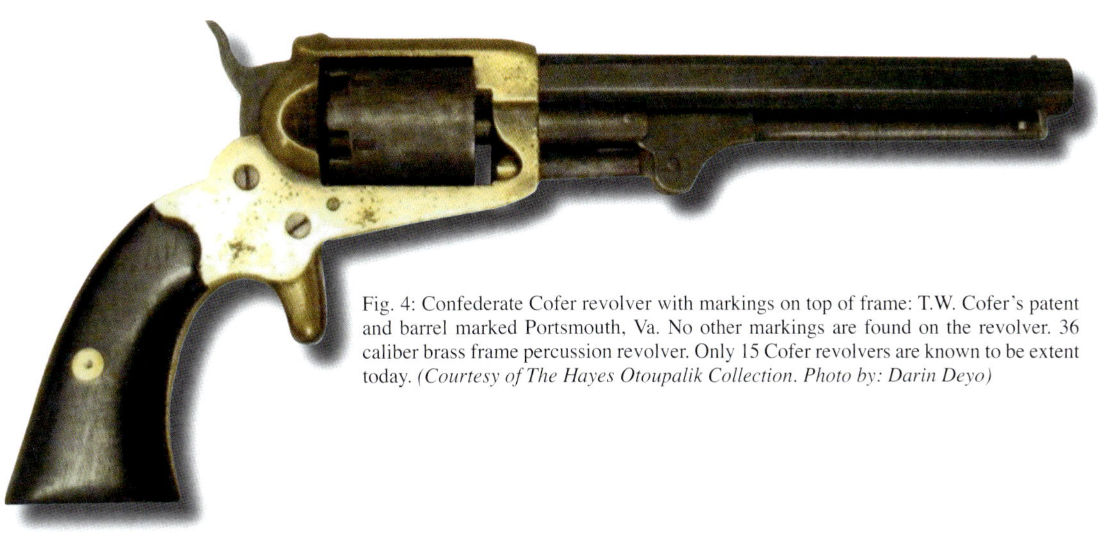

Fig. 4: Confederate Cofer revolver with markings on top of frame: T.W. Cofer's patent and barrel marked Portsmouth, Va. No other markings are found on the revolver. 36 caliber brass frame percussion revolver. Only 15 Cofer revolvers are known to be extent today. *(Courtesy of The Hayes Otoupalik Collection. Photo by: Darin Deyo)*

Fig. 5: *(Courtesy of The Hayes Otoupalik Collection. Photo by: Darin Deyo)*

Other Whitney Copies

Occasionally other revolvers are seen that are obviously patterned after Whitney's revolvers.

The following revolvers should also be acknowledged as bearing similarities to the revolvers of Eli Whitney, Jr.

Shawk & McLanahan Navy Model Revolver

Although the Shawk & McLanahan revolver is not considered a Confederate revolver, it is a pre-war revolver that is very similar to the First Model Whitney Navy Revolver. These revolvers were manufactured around 1858 in Carondelet, St. Louis, MO. Approximately 100 of these revolvers were produced by Union sympathizers William Shawk of Pennsylvania and J.K. McLanahan of Ohio.[9]

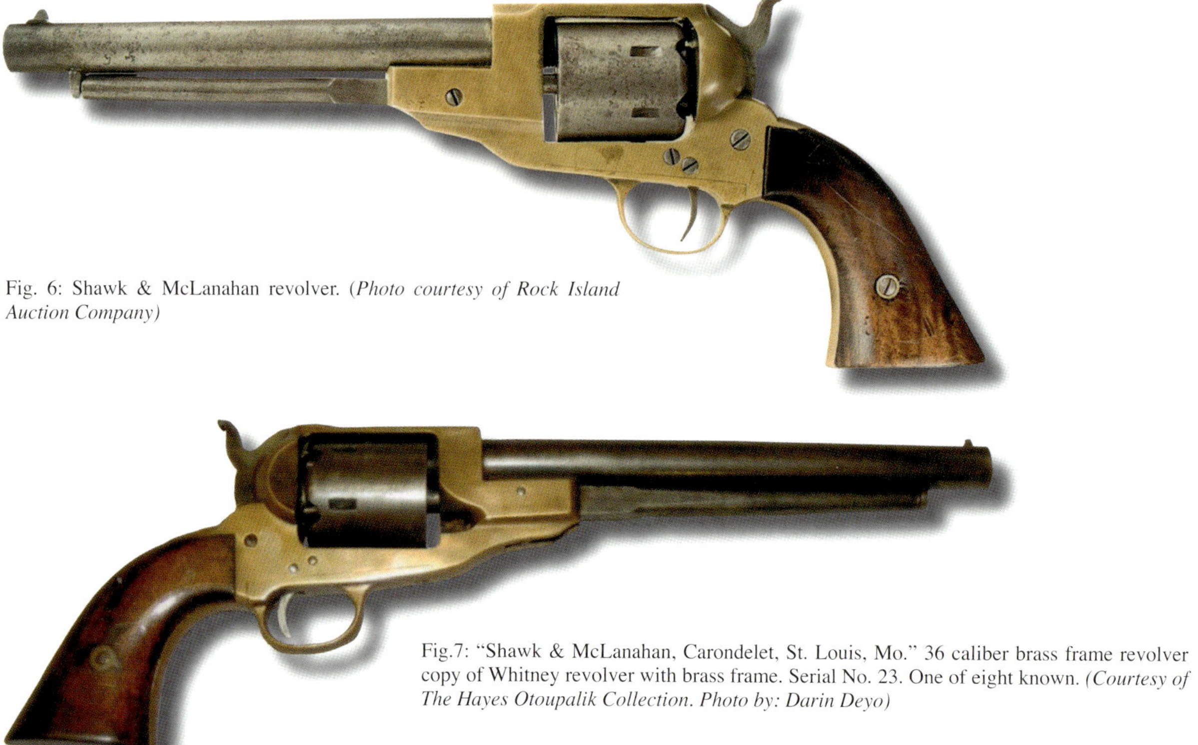

Fig. 6: Shawk & McLanahan revolver. *(Photo courtesy of Rock Island Auction Company)*

Fig.7: "Shawk & McLanahan, Carondelet, St. Louis, Mo." 36 caliber brass frame revolver copy of Whitney revolver with brass frame. Serial No. 23. One of eight known. *(Courtesy of The Hayes Otoupalik Collection. Photo by: Darin Deyo)*

W.W. Marston

Barrels were marked with the trade names *Union Arms Co.* or *Western Arms Co.* The cylinders may have been made by Whitney, as some bore the same cylinder scene as Whitney's revolvers. Manufactured in the late 1850s to early 1860s.[10]

Fig. 8: W.W. Marston revolver with "*The Union Arms Company*" barrel address. *(Photo courtesy of James D. Julia Auctioneers)*

William Irving of New York

William Irving was perhaps an agent for both W.W. Marston and James Reid, also of New York City. A Second Model pocket revolver bearing his name and address is similar to Whitney's Pocket revolver.[11]

Fig. 9: *(Courtesy of The Hayes Otoupalik Collection. Photo by: Darin Deyo)*

Three westerners. The close up of photo indicates a metallic cartridge revolver with Whitney characteristics (two piece grip, top strap). Many revolvers were converted to cartridge following the Civil War, for use on the American frontier. (*Courtesy Denis Gaubert*)

8

WHITNEY NAVY CONVERSIONS

Within the decade following the War Between the States, percussion firearms were rapidly becoming outdated, as manufacturers began producing weapons that used a self contained cartridge. Many of the percussion revolvers that had provided such reliable service during the War were converted to accept these new cartridges. The Whitney Navy revolver is sometimes found among that group of revolvers that we call "Conversions." Some arms manufacturers converted their percussion arms at their manufacturing facility, while other arms were converted by unknown gunsmiths elsewhere. It is believed that very few, if any, of the Whitney conversions were products of the Whitney Arms Company.[1]

Eli Whitney, Jr. would certainly have been capable of converting percussion revolvers to cartridge revolvers. Whitney had been granted U.S. Patent No. 51,985 on January 9, 1866, for a metallic cartridge revolver. This revolver used a cylinder cap that also served as a cartridge extractor. Although this patent was not for the purpose of converting revolvers, it would indicate Whitney possessed the ability to do so. Unfortunately, there is no evidence that this metallic cartridge revolver was ever manufactured, and there are no records of any conversions that were done by Whitney.[2] The patent for a metallic cartridge revolver meant Whitney had ceased, or would soon cease, production of his percussion revolver. The Whitney revolvers that were to become conversions were already in use. The author located 16 conversion revolvers during this study. All were Second Model, 4th Types, and were found in the 19000 through 27000 serial number ranges. Often these revolvers were found bearing the markings of the U.S. Navy.

The Navy retained Whitney revolvers in their inventory until 1873, when they began selling their surplus small arms and ammunition at auction. That year at least 2,000 Whitney revolvers were sold to Mr. J.W. Frazier of New York at a price of $1.57 each. Another bid to purchase all surplus revolvers at the Pensacola Navy Yard was submitted by Mr. James D. Kenney. He purchased the Whitney revolvers at a price of $2.20 each. In 1875, the last lot of 271 revolvers were sold to Ellis F. Armstrong of Vallejo, California.[3] No doubt, many of these surplus revolvers were converted to metallic cartridge, plated with nickel, and sold on the civilian market.

There is a group of Whitney Navy revolvers that were converted by using the same basic method as that found on the Remington New Model Army revolver conversions. These revolvers indicate a more professional workmanship than some of the other conversions encountered. They are marked with a conversion number or assembly number, indicating the process was done at the same factory. The cylinder is made from two pieces. The rear of the cylinder is cut off down to the ratchet shaft and an extension added. The extension is brazed to the cylinder and the six chambers are bored through. The rear of the chambers are counter bored for the cartridge flanges. A backing plate (approximately 0.085 inch thick) is dovetailed into the rear of the frame, and the nose of the hammer is reshaped. A loading channel is milled through the right side of the recoil shield.[4]

Examples of revolvers that were converted in this manner are shown in Figures 1, 2, and 3.

Figure 1 below shows a Whitney Conversion, serial number 19422, without Naval markings. This revolver bears a conversion number "49" and retains most of its nickel plating.

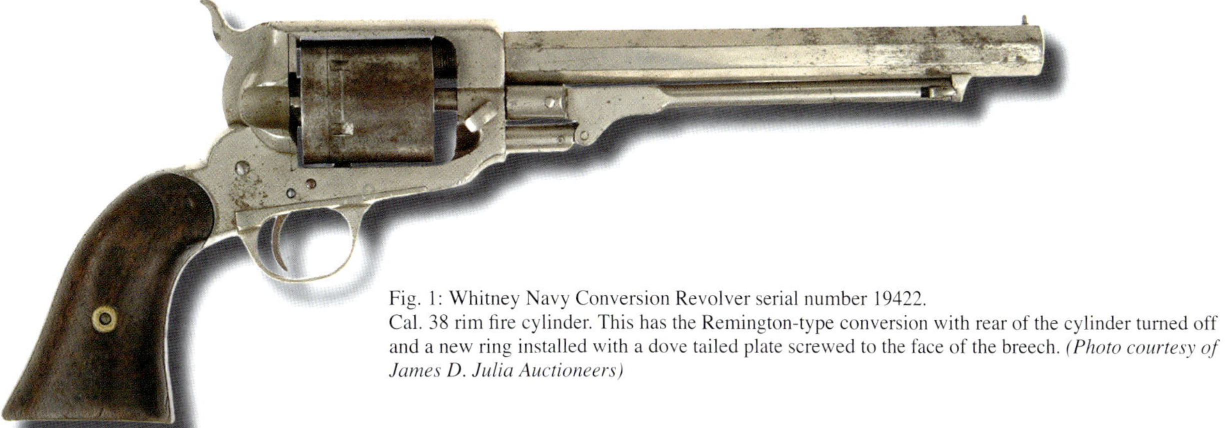

Fig. 1: Whitney Navy Conversion Revolver serial number 19422.
Cal. 38 rim fire cylinder. This has the Remington-type conversion with rear of the cylinder turned off and a new ring installed with a dove tailed plate screwed to the face of the breech. *(Photo courtesy of James D. Julia Auctioneers)*

The revolver in Figure 2 bears a conversion number "40" and retains about 40% of its nickel plating. It is serial number 22315 and does not have any Naval markings.

Fig. 2: Whitney Navy Conversion Revolver serial number 22315. Remington type conversion with dovetailed plate on the recoil shield. *(Photo courtesy of James D. Julia Auctioneers)*

The revolver pictured below, serial number 24283, is an example of a former Naval revolver that has been converted to cartridge and nickel plated. Converted in the same fashion as the above revolvers, it bears the conversion (assembly) number "9."

Fig. 3: Whitney Navy Conversion Revolver serial number 24283 Cal. 38 Rim Fire Conversion appears to be the standard Remington type, but the ratchet ring on the back of the cylinder has a double ring with a lower edge on the inside. There is an anchor on the top of the barrel and the periphery of the cylinder. In addition to the anchors there is a heavy "US" on top of the barrel. About 2/3 of the nickel finish remains. *(Photo and description courtesy of James D. Julia Auctioneers)*

Fig. 4: The anchor and the "US" stamp on the barrel of Whitney revolver serial number 24283 indicate this revolver was once in the inventory of the U.S. Navy. *(Photo courtesy of James D. Julia Auctioneers)*

The following Whitney revolver, serial number 25539, was not nickel plated and does not bear a conversion (or assembly) number. The conversion method differs in cylinder construction, shape of the hammer nose, and the lack of a cylinder backing plate. The chambers were not counter bored for cartridge flanges.[5]

The number of Whitney revolvers that were converted to cartridge is unknown. Also, the final destinations of these firearms are unknown, but no doubt, many were used on the Western frontier. These surplus revolvers that became nickel plated conversions were quite possibly sold to settlers and cowboys who needed reliable handguns. They would have been less expensive than the new metallic cartridge revolvers of Colt, Remington, or Smith & Wesson. In addition, some of these conversions allowed for the use of a percussion cylinder as well as a metallic cartridge cylinder. This feature would have been very useful when the owner had no ready access to the new metallic cartridges.

The metallic cartridge conversion revolvers of that period played a unique role in history, and the Whitney Navy revolver was among that special group.

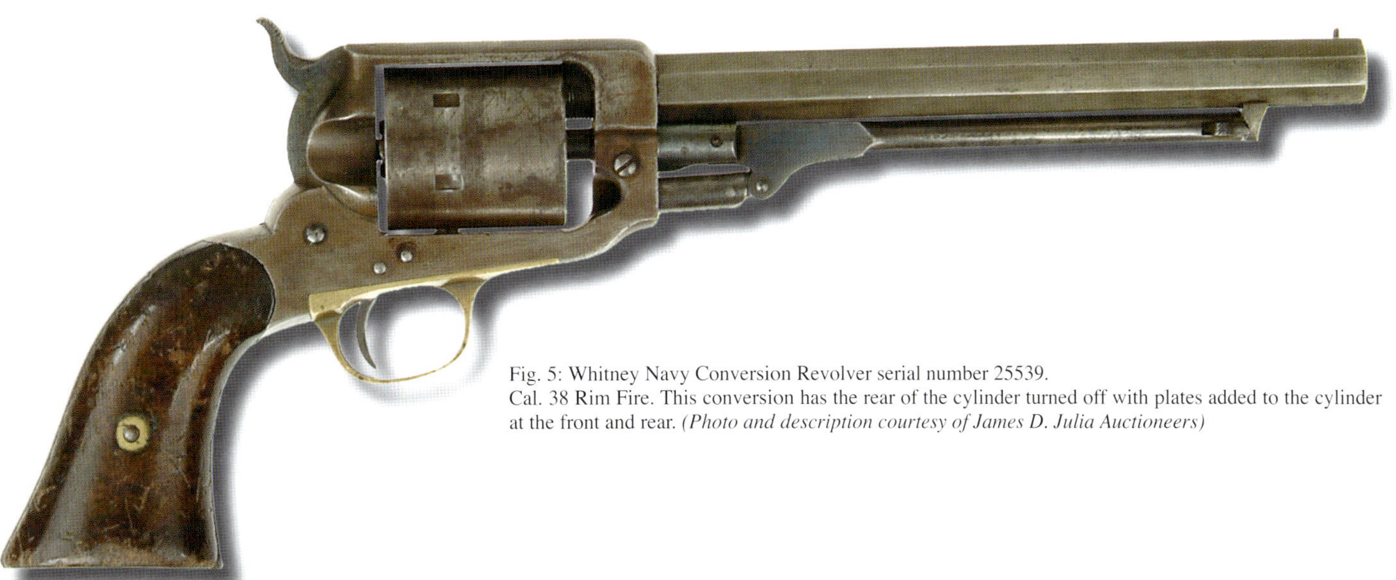

Fig. 5: Whitney Navy Conversion Revolver serial number 25539.
Cal. 38 Rim Fire. This conversion has the rear of the cylinder turned off with plates added to the cylinder at the front and rear. *(Photo and description courtesy of James D. Julia Auctioneers)*

This engraved Whitney Navy revolver is displayed in a modern mahogany case. The interior is purple velvet lined and compartmented in bottom for revolver, a large Navy/Army single sided flask with Trophy of Arms decoration and crossed pistols & rifles above; a Whitney 2-cavity bullet & ball mold with sprue cutter; an L-shaped nipple wrench; a small English pewter oil bottle; a tin of Goldmark's caps and a functioning key. *(Photo and description courtesy of James D. Julia Auctioneers)*

9

ENGRAVED WHITNEYS AND IVORY GRIPS

Factory engraved Whitney revolvers are scarce. In *Flayderman's Guide to Antique American Firearms*, Norm Flayderman states that considering the large numbers of handguns made by Whitney, there are surprisingly few found with extra features, such as engraving or fancy grips. He adds, "Engraving on percussion handguns is rarely seen, although some specimens are known."[1]

The author found this to be case, as only a few revolvers having extra features were found during this study. However, we do know that Whitney advertised these extra features as early as January 1860. In his price list from that year Whitney offers "Ivory Stock for Belt and Holster Pistol" for an additional $6.00. He also includes "Ornamental engraving on Belt and Holster Pistols" for an additional $5.00.

There were three revolvers noted during the research for this book which were blued with ivory grips. The earliest was serial number 2916. This was a well used revolver with aging ivory grips. The grips were unnumbered. The second was a very pristine revolver with matching factory ivory grips. This revolver, serial number 4249, is pictured below. The third revolver, serial number 5639, was pictured in Chapter Five, Martial Whiteys. That revolver has ivory grips with the names of battles engraved on the grips. The author was unable to determine if those grips were numbered to the revolver.

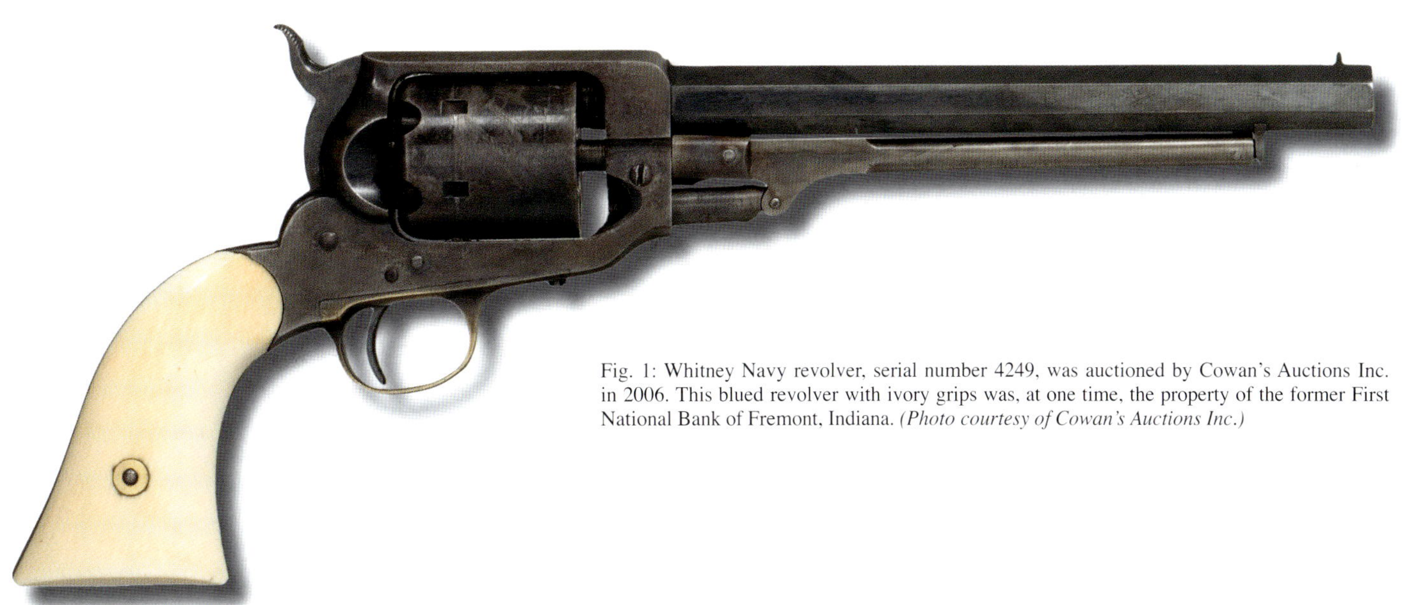

Fig. 1: Whitney Navy revolver, serial number 4249, was auctioned by Cowan's Auctions Inc. in 2006. This blued revolver with ivory grips was, at one time, the property of the former First National Bank of Fremont, Indiana. *(Photo courtesy of Cowan's Auctions Inc.)*

The author located three examples of engraved Whitney revolvers. The best example was one that had been sold by James D. Julia Auctioneers of Fairfield, Maine. This revolver, serial number 19882, is pictured in Figures 2, 3, and 4 below.

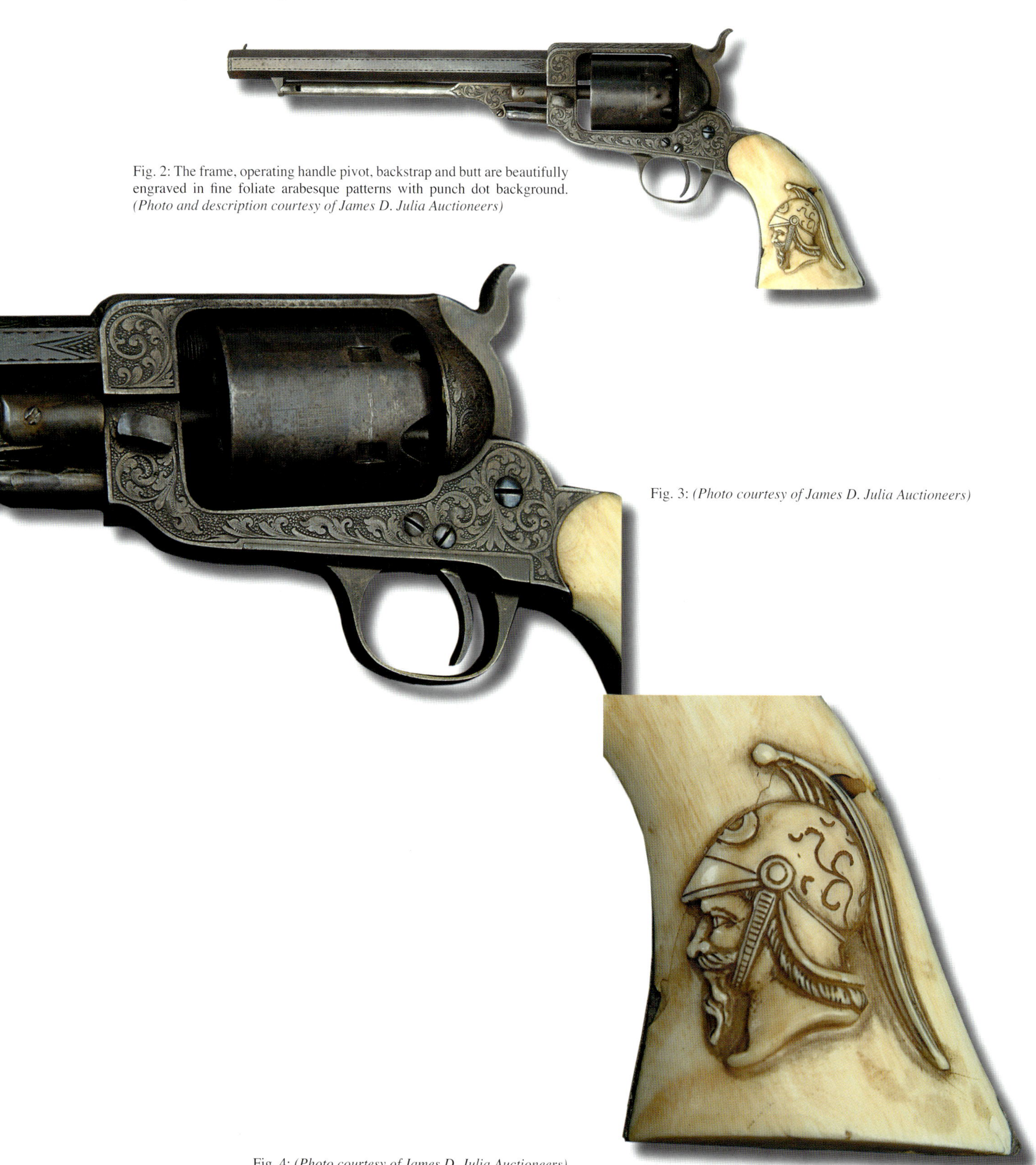

Fig. 2: The frame, operating handle pivot, backstrap and butt are beautifully engraved in fine foliate arabesque patterns with punch dot background. *(Photo and description courtesy of James D. Julia Auctioneers)*

Fig. 3: *(Photo courtesy of James D. Julia Auctioneers)*

Fig. 4: *(Photo courtesy of James D. Julia Auctioneers)*

Another engraved Whitney Navy revolver is serial number 7960. This example was also found in the listings of James D. Julia Auctioneers of Fairfield, Maine. It was noted that this revolver has very old replacement smooth ivory grips.

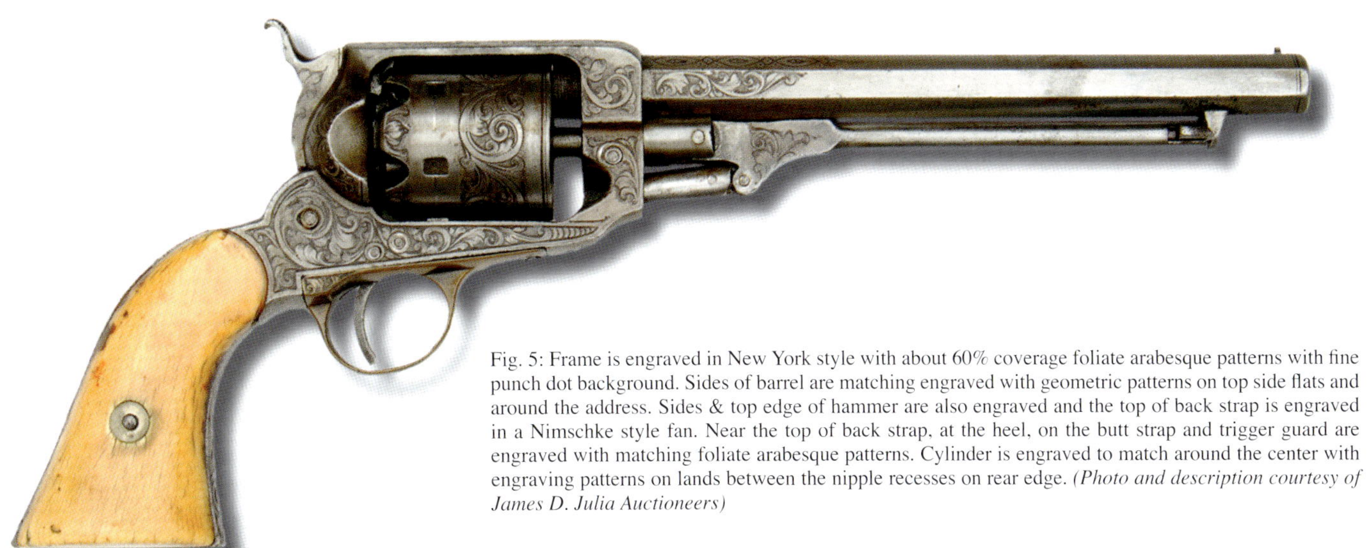

Fig. 5: Frame is engraved in New York style with about 60% coverage foliate arabesque patterns with fine punch dot background. Sides of barrel are matching engraved with geometric patterns on top side flats and around the address. Sides & top edge of hammer are also engraved and the top of back strap is engraved in a Nimschke style fan. Near the top of back strap, at the heel, on the butt strap and trigger guard are engraved with matching foliate arabesque patterns. Cylinder is engraved to match around the center with engraving patterns on lands between the nipple recesses on rear edge. *(Photo and description courtesy of James D. Julia Auctioneers)*

Fig. 6: Hand engraved "*E. WHITNEY N. HAVEN, U.S.A.*" barrel address. *(Photo courtesy of James D. Julia Auctioneers)*

The third example of an engraved revolver is serial number 4771. This revolver is also pictured on page 288 of *Civil War Guns* by William B. Edwards. Edwards indicates that this revolver's engraving is "much worn and plated over but may be original with period of gun's use. Grips are pearl."[2]

The barrel address is the original first type "E. Whitney / N. Haven" address, which may indicate the revolver was engraved after leaving the factory: see Figure 8.

Fig. 7: *(Photo courtesy Emery Henderson)*

Fig. 8: *(Photo courtesy Emery Henderson)*

Fig. 9: *(Photo courtesy Emery Henderson)*

Fig. 10: *(Photo courtesy Emery Henderson)*

A Word about Cased Revolvers

One would expect to find some of these engraved revolvers "cased" in wood boxes with accoutrements. Some may have been originally sold in cases, but none were found during the author's research. Without doubt there were some Whitney Navy revolvers that were cased. However, the number of these revolvers would certainly have been far fewer than Colt or Remington revolvers, making "cased" Whitney revolvers rare. Only 34,000 Whitney Navy revolvers were produced, and approximately half of that number were sold to the military and would not have been cased. Only one revolver was located during this study that appeared to be a period cased revolver. This was a presentation to a Union officer that was made during, or perhaps after, the Civil War. When it was cased, and who provided the case, is unknown. Cases were supplied by various dealers to revolver manufacturers. Even Colt, who provided many sets of cased revolvers, had cases made on contract by different dealers. In addition, the private dealers who bought firearms from the manufacturers could have had cases made by local craftsmen.[3]

Whitney did, of course, include the accoutrements with his revolvers. His price list of January 1860 lists his revolver with "Bullet Mould, Nipple Wrench and Screw-driver." In addition, a powder flask could be purchased for $1.00.

The only other cased revolvers located by the author were Whitney Pocket revolvers. One of these was pictured in *The Whitney Firearms* by Claud Fuller, and was a presentation to its owner by a member of the Whitney family. Another cased Pocket revolver was sold in 2006 by Greg Martin Auctions.

TABLE OF BRITISH POSSESSIONS
BRITISH
EMPIRE
throughout the
WORLD
TABLE OF BRITISH POSSESSIONS
A. FULLARTON & Co. EDINBURGH, LONDON & DUBLIN.

10

WHITNEYS IN FOREIGN SERVICE

A few of the Whitney Navy revolvers that were encountered during this study bore the markings of other countries. Whitney revolvers were among those sold to foreign nations during the years following the Civil War. There was a surplus of weapons after the Civil War, and even more percussion firearms would become available for sale as the development of cartridge guns made them obsolete. Some of these percussion weapons were disposed of as surplus during the Franco-Prussian War (1870-71), as well as during other foreign conflicts. Two contributors to this book, one in Peru and one in Chile, reported finding surplus arms in South America. Both individuals own Whitney revolvers in the 28000 serial number range. These weapons were believed to have been used in The War of the Pacific (1879-83), involving the countries of Chile, Peru, and Bolivia.

The author was unable to locate any records of sales made by Whitney to foreign nations. The Whitney Navy revolvers were out of production by the late 1860s, and it is likely that private dealers had purchased some of the surplus arms, and perhaps some of Whitney's final inventory, to sell overseas. Great Britain purchased surplus weapons, often for use in its colonies. A revolver that bears London proof marks, and two other revolvers that saw service with the police force of South Australia appear on the following pages.

Many surplus American weapons were sold to foreign countries following the American Civil War. Some countries, such as Great Britain, applied their stamps indicating the weapon had been inspected and proofed. (*Author's collection*)

Facing page: Great Britain acquired both new and surplus firearms from the United States. Shown on the map of the British Empire in the 1850s, by John Bartholomew, is a Whitney revolver with British proof marks. (*Revolver courtesy of George Tondryk*)

Great Britain

This revolver is a 5th Type Whitney revolver with the large trigger guard bearing the London proof and view marks on the cylinder and barrel flat. This revolver is also reported as having seven groove barrel rifling.

Fig. 1: Whitney Navy revolver serial number 32862, with London proof marks. *(Courtesy of George Tondryk)*

Fig. 2: Proof mark on cylinder. *(Courtesy of George Tondryk)*

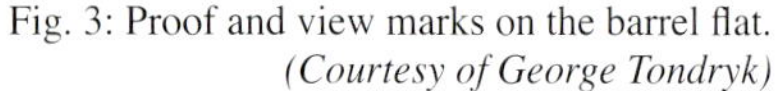

Fig. 3: Proof and view marks on the barrel flat. *(Courtesy of George Tondryk)*

Australia

Three revolvers were located that had the markings of the South Australian police. All were Second Model, 4th Type Navy revolvers in the 26000-27000 serial number range. These revolvers are pictured in this section.

The Powerhouse Museum of Sidney, Australia, also has Whitney Navy revolver #22774 in its collection. This revolver bears the inspection mark "*FCW*" (Frank C. Warner, who inspected revolvers for the U.S. Navy in 1864). This may well have been a surplus revolver purchased at auction in the 1870s and sold overseas.

There was one other revolver in the author's study that was reported as having been used by an individual on the Australian frontier during the late 1800s. That revolver was in the low 27000 serial number range, and did not have police markings.

These revolvers represent a few of the purchases by Great Britain and her colonies during the years following the American Civil War.

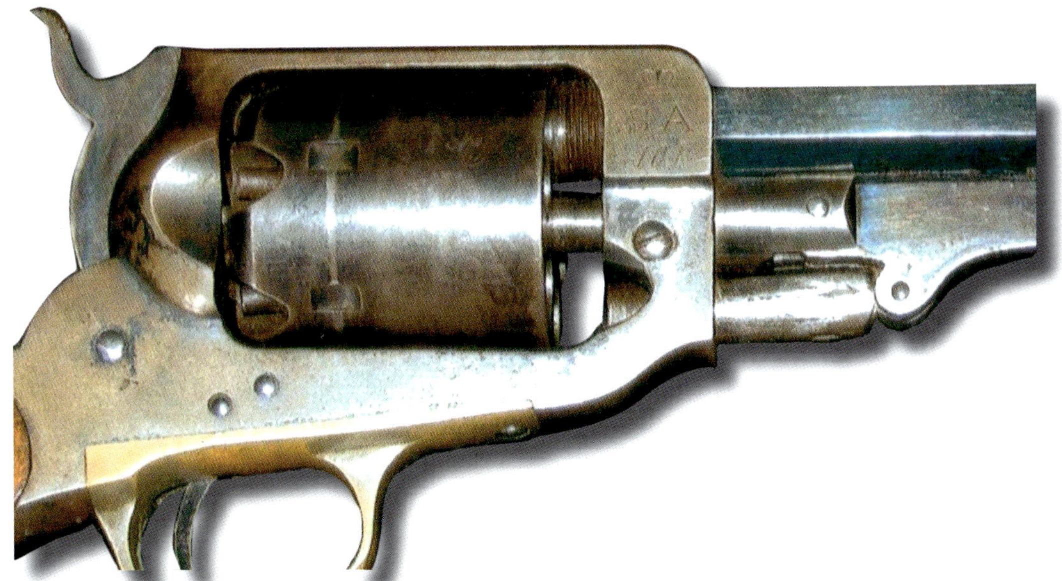

Fig. 4: Whitney Navy revolver serial number 26541, bearing South Australian police markings. A "Crown / SA / 101" is stamped on the right frame. *(Courtesy of Neil Kenney)*

Fig. 5: Whitney Navy revolver serial number 26541 used by the South Australian police. (*Courtesy of Neil Kenney*)

Fig. 6: Whitney Navy revolver serial number 27488 used by the South Australian police (*Courtesy of the Powerhouse Museum Collection, Sydney. Photo by: Sotha Bourn*)

Fig. 7: Whitney Navy revolver serial number 27488, bearing South Australian police markings. A "Crown / SA / 81" is stamped on the right frame. (*Courtesy of the Powerhouse Museum Collection, Sydney. Photo by: Sotha Bourn*)

Fig. 8: Whitney Navy revolver serial number 26062. South Australian police markings. "Crown / SA / 121" stamped on right frame. *(Courtesy of Brian Dunn)*

Fig. 9: *(Courtesy of Brian Dunn)*

War of the Pacific (1879-83)

The War of the Pacific was fought in western South America from 1879 to 1883, with the country of Chile fighting against Peru and Bolivia. Whitney revolvers were among the surplus weapons from the United States that found their way into this conflict. The two revolvers shown below saw service during that period.

There were many countries using surplus firearms from America during the late 1800s, and numerous conflicts were fought throughout the world. The revolvers shown in this Chapter represent the role of the Whitney Navy Revolver in world events during the period following the American Civil War.

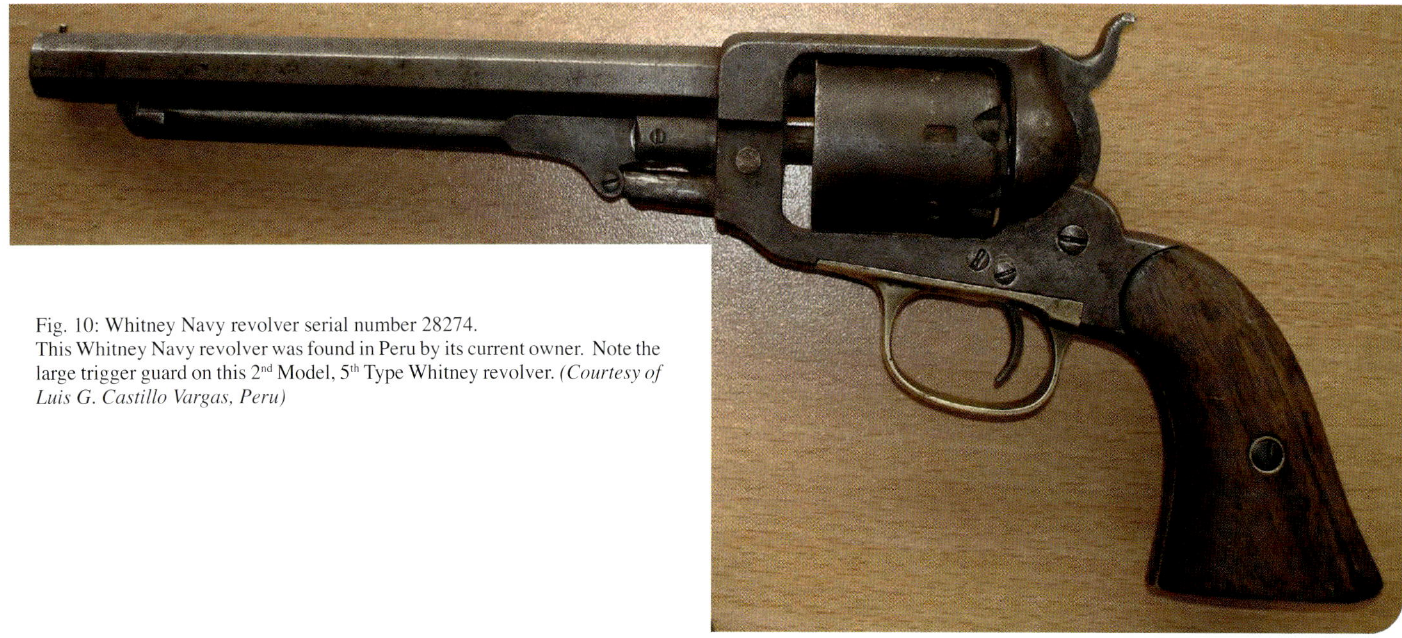

Fig. 10: Whitney Navy revolver serial number 28274.
This Whitney Navy revolver was found in Peru by its current owner. Note the large trigger guard on this 2nd Model, 5th Type Whitney revolver. *(Courtesy of Luis G. Castillo Vargas, Peru)*

Fig. 11: Whitney Navy revolver serial number 28675.
This Whitney Navy revolver was found in Santiago, Chile by its current owner in 1979. *(Courtesy of H.W. Goldsmith, Santiago, Chile)*

CONCLUSION

The Whitney Navy revolver, with its solid frame, simple construction, and sleek lines, is a classic revolver. With possibly 1,500 First Models and only about 34,000 Second Models produced, the Whitney Navy revolver is rare when compared to the number of Colt and Remington revolvers of the period. Although limited in number, these revolvers may still occasionally be found. Collecting the Whitney Navy revolver can present a challenge to collectors, as some "types" of the Second Model are easily found, while other variations are scarce. All "types" of the First Model are prized by collectors.

The author began his research of the Whitney Navy revolver with the objective of learning more about this revolver while verifying the serial number ranges of each type. After reviewing and compiling data on 370 Whitney Navy revolvers, it became obvious that the serial number ranges assigned to each "type" of the Second Model needed revision. Data obtained for the First Model Whitney Navy revolver was limited and suggested only one minor adjustment to previously published data. The author acknowledges that there may be exceptions to the results of this study. As with any firearms research, "all of the guns have not yet been seen."

It is the hope of the author that the results of this study, and the contents of this book, will be of benefit to all who have an interest in historic firearms, and to all collectors of the finest revolver manufactured by Eli Whitney, Jr., *The Whitney Navy Revolver.*

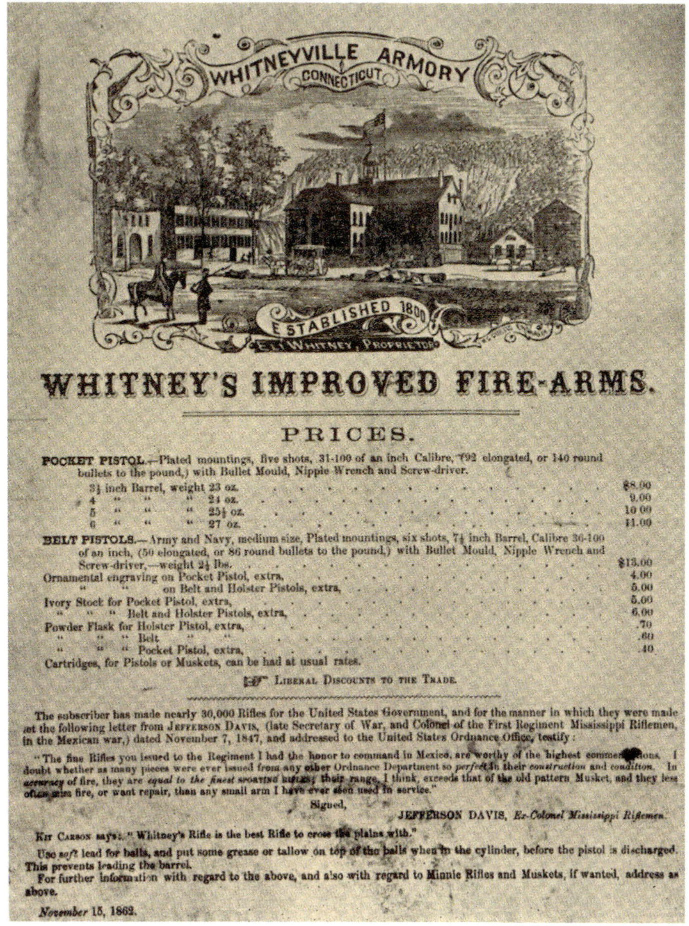

Whitney Firearms advertisement dated November 15, 1862. *(Original image appeared in The Whitney Firearms by Claud E. Fuller, 1946)*

APPENDIX

APPENDIX A: SERIAL NUMBERS

Serial numbers of Whitney Navy revolvers tested by the Navy Ordnance Yard in Washington City, February 12, 1864.

22014	22158	23001
22015	22176	23004
22021	22178	23013
22024	22184	23014
22037	22251	23021
22044	22256	23025
22045	22267	23026
22058	22276	23029
22068	22277	23031
22076	22279	23034
22078	22287	23035
22086	22294	23045
22096	22360	23375
22150	22381	

Serial numbers of Whitney Navy revolvers tested by the Navy Ordnance Yard in Washington City on December 8, 1864. [Serial number 25443 was listed twice in the original report.]

25371	26233	26404	26532
25400	26237	26405	26536
25443	26240	26408	26540
26001	26244	26409	26549
26002	26246	26411	26551
26004	26295	26413	26553
26006	26301	26414	26559
26007	26304	26415	26560
26009	26307	26419	26563
26017	26308	26421	26569
26020	26309	26423	26570
26023	26310	26425	26576
26028	26318	26427	26578
26035	26320	26429	26584
26038	26321	26430	26585
26040	26323	26432	26586
26044	26327	26436	26587
26045	26328	26437	26590
26167	26340	26439	26591
26191	26341	26442	26592
26203	26342	26444	26593
26210	26344	26448	26594
26219	26346	26503	26596
26222	26349	26504	26600
26228	26402	26518	

APPENDIX B: ESTIMATED SERIAL NUMBER RANGES BY DATE

There are no known records of the Whitney Arms Company that provide dates of manufacture by serial number ranges.

However, as research was conducted and survey data obtained for this book, the author could not help but speculate as to the dates of manufacture of Whitney revolvers. Many contributors to this study also asked about possible dates of manufacture for the Whitney revolvers in their possession. Therefore, the author decided to share his "estimate" of the dates of manufacture and the facts upon which this analysis is based.

During the writing of this book the author was contacted by Mr. Peter Schiffers, author of a new book titled *Civil War Carbines: Myth vs. Reality*, published by Mowbray Publishing, 54 E. School St, Woonsocket, RI, 02895. Mr. Schiffers and the author compared notes and thoughts on approximate serial number ranges for the Whitney revolvers. The following is this author's "best estimate" of those dates and serial number ranges, and the information on which those estimates are based. Whitney did not always ship revolvers based on a "first manufactured – first shipped" method; however, it is believed this analysis will provide approximate dates for various serial ranges.

1857 - 1858	# 1 - 1000 (First Model)
1859	# 1000 - 1500 (end First Model) and # 1 - 600 (Second Model)
1860	# 600 - 2500
1861	# 2500 - 7500
1862	# 7500 - 17500
1863	# 17500 - 22500
1864	# 22500 - 28500
1865 - 1866	# 28500 - 34000

Analysis:

1857 - 1858: Between November 1857 and January 1858, Whitney offered to furnish 300 Colt Navy revolvers, or some of his "own models," to the Navy. Therefore, he must have begun manufacture of his own revolvers as Colt's patent expired in 1857. The author believes a few hundred revolvers were made in 1857, with the majority of the First Model production occurring in 1858.

1859: Whitney's price list to the Ordnance Department, dated January 1860, specifies "plated mountings" (see Chapter Five). Although he could have applied silver plating to some of the iron-trigger guards of the First Models, the author is of the opinion this practice began with the brass trigger guards of the Second Model. Whitney's letter dated June 16, 1859 (see Chapter Five), also indicates a "New Model" to be manufactured in 1859. The author believes this "New Model" to be the "Second Model" Whitney.

1860: As the South began arming for war, Maryland purchased 1,000 Whitney revolvers and Virginia purchased at least 500. Reference was made in Virginia correspondence regarding the need for safety "pins" on Whitney revolvers, and in a later letter that the safety pin issue had been corrected. Possibly the "improved revolver" (with safety slot) was already available when the first reference was written, and within a month it was reported that the Whitney cylinders had been "improved" (see Chapter Six). Early Second Models were already available at the beginning of 1860.

1861: The U.S. Army purchased 1,281 Whitney revolvers from several private dealers between August and December. It is likely that these dealers had begun purchasing firearms from numerous manufacturers in 1860 as war tensions increased.

1862: Martially marked revolvers in the early 11000 serial range (and possibly earlier) had a cylinder scene containing naval ships and an ironclad monitor. Since the USS *Monitor* was introduced in 1862, and the first ironclad battle occurred in March 1862, these revolvers were manufactured after that date. Whitney received a contract with the U.S. Army in June for 7,000 revolvers. He immediately began production and delivery. The Army purchased approximately 5,600 revolvers from Whitney during 1862, and another 811 from private companies. Whitney stated in a letter dated January 28, 1863 (see Chapter Five), that he was manufacturing 1,000 revolvers per month to supply the Army contract.

1863: We know from deliveries to the Army and Navy that some 4,600 revolvers were shipped. Whitney's contract with the Army ceased in early 1863; however, his contract with the Navy began about the same time, this being the mid period of the Civil War. Whitney was probably shipping everything to the military in efforts to keep up with purchase orders. One of the revolvers sent to the Navy in January 1863 was serial number 17751 (mentioned in a letter dated February 4, 1863, from Lieutenant Commander Skerett). Later in the year Whitney received orders for muskets, with approximately 1,500 muskets being purchased from him during the last few months of 1863.

1864: The "FCW" marked revolvers (approximate serial numbered range 22500-24000) were inspected in early 1864. The last shipment inspected by the Navy in December 1864 included serial number 26600 (the highest number in the list of those revolvers inspected). There were two more shipments of 200 revolvers in 1864, which pushed the serial number range to 26800. Whitney was trying to keep up with orders during this period, and it is believed that most of his production was going directly to the military. (In addition to his revolver production efforts, approximately 11,000 muskets were purchased from Whitney during the year).

Whitney stated in June 1864 that he would begin manufacturing revolvers with the larger trigger guards. He may have begun this in late 1864; however, none that we recorded in the survey were noted as being martially marked. According to the survey, the larger trigger guards appeared around serial number 28000. As orders with the Navy began to decline, it is likely that sales to private dealers and individuals continued.

1865 - 1866: As the War ended, so did Whitney's revolver contracts. Several relic Whitney revolvers included in this survey may provide some evidence that these revolvers were still being acquired by individuals and used during the last days of the War. Two relic revolvers in the 30000 serial number range, and one in the 28000 range, would indicate production and use in early 1865. In addition, a revolver in the 28000 serial range was noted as having Naval inspector's initials on the cylinder. The remainder of the Whitney Navy revolvers were probably produced by the end of 1866 or early 1867. Some of these Whitney revolvers very likely found their way to the American frontier, while others were sold overseas.

APPENDIX C: IDENTIFIED WHITNEY REVOLVERS

Some Interesting and Famous Whitney Revolvers

Whitney Navy revolver # 152 used by a frontier scout
This revolver, purchased by its current owner at an arms fair in England, is inscribed "J. Peate" on the side of the loading lever and "Blue Hills & Kans." inside the grips. James (Jack) Peate was a scout, dispatch rider, and cowboy. His exploits as a dispatch rider in the Blue Hills area of Kansas during an indian ambush in 1866, and frontier scout for the 10th Cavalry in 1868, were documented by Mr. Slim Ackerman in the magazine *Muzzle Blasts*, June 1982. Peate later became president of the Beverly State Bank in Kansas and died in 1932. *(Courtesy of Mr. William Upton)*

Whitney Navy revolver # 1599
Engraved on trigger guard "*Lt Col Samuel T. Harison.*" *(Virginia Historical Society)*

Whitney Navy revolver # 2255
Etched on several locations of this revolver is "*J.S.G. Gay, Winchester Ky.*" Research indicates this was Jonathan Stamper Gardner Gay, a Captain in the 8th Kentucky Cavalry, CSA, serving under General John Hunt Morgan. Gay was taken prisoner during Morgan's raid into Ohio and held as prisoner for two years at Johnson's Island, Ohio (revolver is pictured in Chapter Six). *(Courtesy of Mr. James A. Rogers)*

Whitney Navy revolver # 2796
Used by Bishop Alfred Magill Randolph, who served as a Confederate Army chaplain. *(Museum of the Confederacy)*

Whitney Navy revolver # 2814
Used by Commodore William F. Lynch, CSN. He served as a Captain in the Virginia Navy and then in the Confederate States Navy. *(Museum of the Confederacy)*

Whitney Navy revolver # 3110
General JEB Stuart, Commander of the Confederate Cavalry Corp, used this revolver (revolver is pictured in Chapter Six). *(Virginia Historical Society)*

Whitney Navy revolver # 3826
Inscribed to Confederate *Colonel Charles C. Lee, 37th NC Troops* (revolver is pictured in Chapter Six). *(Greg Martin Auctions, November 2005 auction)*

Whitney Navy revolver # 5348
Associated with Henry B. Barber, an enlisted member of Company A, 7th Illinois Cavalry Regiment. *(Little John's Auction Service, May 2011 auction)*

Whitney Navy revolver # 5639
Carried by Colonel Julius Adams, 67th Regiment, New York Infantry. *(West Point Museum)*

Whitney Navy revolver # 67*9 L
Once belonged to the famous Sioux Chief Sitting Bull. *(Cowan's Auctions, Inc., 2005 auction)*

Whitney Navy revolver # 6834
Associated with James W. Sinclair, 43rd Battalion Virginia Cavalry, Mosby's Command (revolver is pictured in Chapter Four). *(Courtesy of Mr. James Hambright)*

Whitney Navy revolver # 10295
Inscribed to Confederate *Lieut.A.G.O'Brien/Co D.13th Miss.Vols. (Amoskeag Auction Company, Inc., May 2011 auction)*

Whitney Navy revolver # 10988
Owned by Hugh C. Cook, an early sheriff of Franklin County, Kansas, and a representative of the 58th District in the 1865 state legislature. He lived until 1901. *(Kansas State Historical Society)*

Whitney Navy revolver # 28619
Associated with Micajah Van Landingham, who served in Company C, 46th Regiment N.C. State Troops. Although this is a later production revolver, it was handed down in the Van Landingham family (revolver pictured in Chapter Four). (*Courtesy of Thomas R. Van Landingham, great grandson of Micajah Van Landingham)*

APPENDIX D: SURVEY FORM USED IN GATHERING DATA

Whitney .36 cal Navy Revolver Survey Questions

1. Please record Serial Number (include any letters that follow or precede serial number) exactly as stamped on the: (you may use an "x" for last digit if you wish, but please include the "letter")
   Loading Lever:___________
   Bottom of Barrel: ___________
   Back of Cylinder (between nipples or ratchet area):____________
   If Trigger Guard is removed:
      Indicate Number/letters on Underside of trigger guard :______________
      On bottom of frame near trigger: _______________
   Inside Grips : Left _________ Right ___________
   Other areas (please indicate location): ___________

2. **Barrel Questions**
   a. Barrel length (measured from muzzle to the cylinder. Include the threaded portion between frame & cylinder) :
      i. 7 5/8 inches ____Yes ____No
      ii. If No, and length appears original, what is the length: _________

   b. Barrel Address is : **(see Reference Sheet for picture)**
      i. ______E. WHITNEY / N. HAVEN
      ii. ______E. WHITNEY / *N. HAVEN* (*N. HAVEN* is slanted)
      iii. ______EAGLE Co.
      iv. ______ None
      v. ______ Other (describe): ______________________________

3. **Does revolver have a Loading Lever** ? ____Yes ____No
   If Yes, please check type of catch (see Reference Sheet for picture).......
   c. _____ Ball type latch at end of loading lever
   b. _____ Colt or "wedge" type latch at end of loading lever
   c. _____ Other, please describe ______________________________

4. **Frame** has : ____ 3 Screws ____ 4 Screws

5. **Trigger Guard** is : _____Brass _____ Iron
   a. Is there any Silvering on trigger guard area: _____Yes ______No

6. **Front sight** is: ___ Pin (post) ____ Dove Tail _____Blade
   ___ Other (describe)_________

7. **Cylinder Questions (see Reference Sheet for Pictures)**
   a. Safety slots on cylinder between nipples:
      ______ One
      ______ Six

   b. Cylinder Scene: _____ Eagle, Shield; and Lion.
      ______ Eagle; Lion; Naval Engagement; and Shield bearing ribbon and marked "Whitneyville".
      ______ Trace of scene but not discernible

______ No visible marking

8. Grips are:

a. ____ Two-piece Wood with Rounded juncture of grip to frame
b. ____ Two-piece Wood with Squared juncture of grip to frame
c. ____ Other type of grip, please describe ____________________________

9. Does revolver have a "Wing-Nut" securing the cylinder pin? ___Yes ___No

a. Is the "Wing-Nut" on the left or right side of frame? ___Left ___Right
b. Does revolver have an **"O"** on frame above the "Wing-nut"? ___Yes ___No
c. Is there an **"O"** on the wing-nut? ___Yes ___No

10. Is your pistol martially marked? ____Yes ____No

<u>Martially Marked Whitneys</u> **(Please answer the following questions if this pistol is martially marked).**

- **Cartouche on Grips:**
  - **a. ____ appears on both grips**
  - **b. ____ left grip only**
  - **c. _____ right grip only**
  - **d. _____ appears to have worn off or sanded off**
  - **e. _____ No cartouche**

- **Inspector & other markings (of <u>martial</u> or <u>non-martial</u> guns) :**
  Please use the following drawings to indicate the location of any markings on your pistol. Record markings exactly as they appear. Please place the appropriate mark on the picture; or draw an arrow to the location & record marking as it appears.

Right Side

Barrel Top (Include any "anchor or US" marks)

Left Side

Trigger guard bottom

Comments:
Please use this space to add any additional comments regarding the above questions; or any other information regarding your pistol.
____
____
____
____

****

Optional:
Name:________________
Address: ____

Phone # : ______________
E-Mail: _________________

If you have pictures you would like to include, please email or mail along with the survey to the address at the bottom of this page. We may use your photos (with credit to you) unless you specify otherwise.

Thank you for your participation in this survey.
We hope this research will provide much needed data regarding the Whitney Navy Revolver, and that a book will be written because of your response. All personal information is confidential.

Completed Surveys may be scanned & returned via e-mail to:
ltdan@whitneyrevolver.com

or by mail to: **Whitney Survey**
c/o Dan Williams
PO Box 55
Beaufort, NC 28516

APPENDIX E: LOST AND FOUND RELIC WHITNEY REVOLVERS

During the course of this project, the author received several survey forms with information about Whitney revolvers that had been recovered from the ground or were "barn or attic" finds. The following are a few of those finds.

Whitney Revolver Serial #106
This Second Model, First Type Whitney revolver, serial number 106, was recovered from the battlefield of Sayler's Creek, Virginia. Fought on April 6, 1865, this was one of the last battles of the War. While there is no proof as to which side lost this revolver, it would seem more likely that it would have been in Confederate hands. It is such an early model Whitney and was still in use during one of the last battles in 1865. Perhaps broken parts caused the revolver to be discarded. *(Courtesy of Colin P. Mahle)*

Whitney Revolver Serial #8197
This martially marked Whitney found in St. Peter, Minnesota, was probably left there by a member of Company B, Minnesota Mounted Rangers which garrisoned the town during the winter of 1862-1863. *(Courtesy of Stephen and Wendy Osman Collection)*

Whitney Revolver Serial #30026
Large trigger guard. Verbal provenance is that this revolver was displayed at the Fort Defiance Museum at Gettysburg, Pennsylvania. *(Courtesy of Colin P. Mahle)*

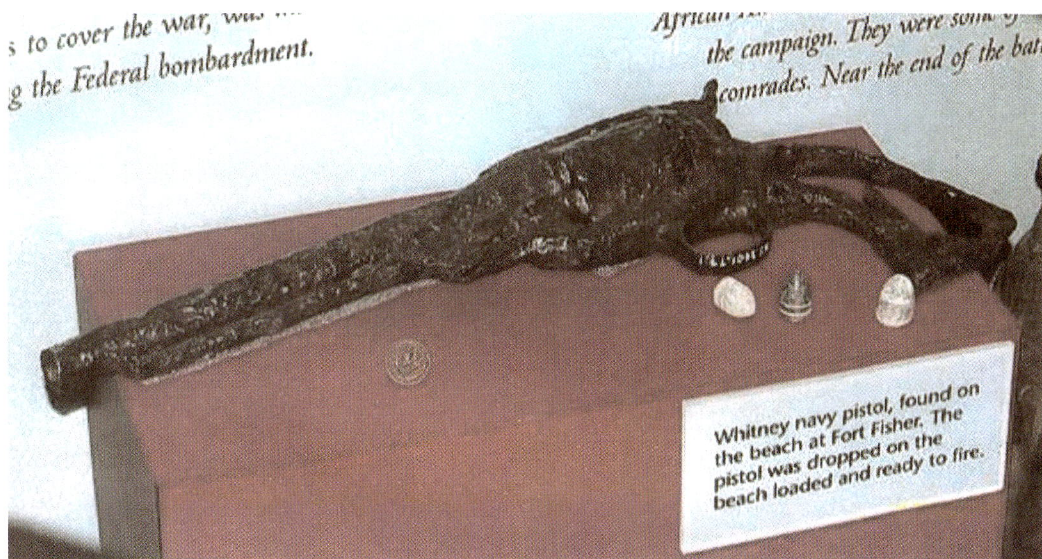

Whitney Revolver Serial number unknown
This Whitney Navy revolver was recovered from the beach near Fort Fisher, NC. The revolver was loaded when lost. The serial number is not visible on this revolver. Fort Fisher fell to Union forces in January 1865. *(Courtesy of the Division of NC State Historic Sites & Properties, Raleigh NC)*

Whitney Revolver Serial number unknown
Relic Whitney Navy revolver with one load still in cylinder and part of one cap still intact on nipple. Revolver came from around Franklin, Tennessee. Serial number is not legible; however, the letters "TD" are visible on the frame. These letters would indicate this revolver was probably in the high 29000 to 32000 serial number range. *(Courtesy of Herman D. Kinder, The Bowling Green Drummer)*

ENDNOTES

Chapter One

1. *The Whitney Firearms.* (Huntington, West Virginia: Standard Publications, Inc., 1946) pg. III
2. *Flayderman's Guide to Antique American Firearms and Their Values.* (Iola, Wisconsin: Gun Digest Books, 2007) pg. 277
3. *The Whitney Firearms.* (Huntington, West Virginia: Standard Publications, Inc., 1946) pg. 171-173
4. *Eli Whitney, The Family.* The Eli Whitney Museum and Workshop, http://www.eliwhitney.org/new/museum/eli-whitney/family.
5. *American Percussion Revolvers.* (Ottawa, Ontario: Museum Restoration Service, 1971) pg. 191-194
6. *Flayderman's Guide to Antique American Firearms and Their Values.* (Iola, Wisconsin: Gun Digest Books, 2007) pg. 294-295
7. *American Percussion Revolvers.* (Ottawa, Ontario: Museum Restoration Service, 1971) pg. 194

Chapter Two

1. *Whitney's Repeating Pistol.* Office of Whitneyville armory price list, submitted to the Ordnance Department, January 1860. Copy obtained from the Texas State Archives.

Chapter Three

1. *The Whitney Firearms.* (Huntington, West Virginia: Standard Publications, Inc., 1946) pg. 310
2. *American Percussion Revolvers.* (Ottawa, Ontario: Museum Restoration Service, 1971) pg. 196

Chapter Four

1. *The Whitney Firearms.* (Huntington, West Virginia: Standard Publications, Inc., 1946) pg. 313

Chapter Five

1. Executive Document No. 99. *Civil War Arms Purchases & Deliveries.* (Lincoln, Rhode Island: Andrew Mowbray Inc. Publishers, 2000)
2. National Archives of the United States, Military Records Department, Washington, D.C., Record Group 74, Records of the Bureau of Ordnance, Entry 5 – "Miscellaneous letters sent. 1853-1867."
3. *Whitney Navy Revolvers.* Chapter 4, unpublished manuscript. Ken Domina and Don Ware.
4. The word "*Colt's*" was struck out by Whitney, apparently giving the Bureau an option on two types of revolvers. *Whitney Navy Revolvers.* Chapter 4, unpublished manuscript. Ken Domina and Don Ware.
5. This theory was based on a similar occurrence with Colt SAA revolvers. *A Study of the Colt Single Action Army Revolver.* (Printed and bound in South Korea: Graphic Publishers, revised fifth printing 2006) pg. 275. Unpublished research records of Ken Domina and Don Ware.
6. National Archives of the United States, Military Records Department, Washington, D.C., Record Group 74, Records of the Bureau of Ordnance, Entry 22 – "Miscellaneous letters sent. 1853-1867." Unpublished research records of Ken Domina and Don Ware.
7. National Archives of the United States, Military Records Department, Washington, D.C., Record Group 74, Records of the Bureau of Ordnance, Entry 5 – "Miscellaneous letters sent. 1853-1867."
8. National Archives of the United States, Military Records Department, Washington, D.C., Record Group 74, Records of the Bureau of Ordnance, Entry 145 – "Correspondence Regarding the Examination of Inventions." Unpublished research records of Ken Domina and Don Ware.

9. Executive Document No. 99. *Civil War Arms Purchases & Deliveries.* (Lincoln, Rhode Island: Andrew Mowbray Inc. Publishers, 2000)
10. National Archives of the United States, Military Records Department, Washington, D.C., Record Group 74, Records of the Bureau of Ordnance, Entry 22 – "Miscellaneous letters sent. 1853-1867." Unpublished research records of Ken Domina and Don Ware.
11. *Civil War Projectiles II Small Arms & Field Artillery.* (Orange, Virginia: Moss Publications 1980) pg. 180
12. National Archives of the United States, Military Records Department, Washington, D.C., Record Group 74, Records of the Bureau of Ordnance, Entry 19 – "Letters received from Navy Yards and Stations." Unpublished research records of Ken Domina and Don Ware.
13. National Archives of the United States, Military Records Department, Washington, D.C., Record Group 74, Records of the Bureau of Ordnance, Entry 19 – "Letters received from Navy Yards and Stations." Unpublished research records of Ken Domina and Don Ware.
14. National Archives of the United States, Military Records Department, Washington, D.C., Record Group 74, Records of the Bureau of Ordnance, Entry 5 – "Miscellaneous letters sent. 1853-1867."
15. *Whitney Navy Revolvers.* Chapter 4, unpublished manuscript. Ken Domina and Don Ware.
16. National Archives of the United States, Military Records Department, Washington, D.C., Record Group 74, Records of the Bureau of Ordnance, Entry 19 – "Letters received from Navy Yards and Stations." Unpublished research records of Ken Domina and Don Ware.
17. National Archives of the United States, Military Records Department, Washington, D.C., Record Group 74, Records of the Bureau of Ordnance, Entry 145 – "Correspondence Regarding the Examination of Inventions." Unpublished research records of Ken Domina and Don Ware.
18. National Archives of the United States, Military Records Department, Washington, D.C., Record Group 74, Records of the Bureau of Ordnance, Entry 22 – "Miscellaneous letters received. 1853-1865." Unpublished research records of Ken Domina and Don Ware.
19. National Archives of the United States, Military Records Department, Washington, D.C., Record Group 74, Records of the Bureau of Ordnance, Entry 19 – "Letters received from Navy Yards and Stations." Unpublished research records of Ken Domina and Don Ware.
20. National Archives of the United States, Military Records Department, Washington, D.C., Record Group 74, Records of the Bureau of Ordnance, Entry 5 - "Miscellaneous letters sent. 1853-1867."
21. "Marking Variations of U.S. Naval Inspectors on Colt 1851 and 1861 Navy Model Revolvers Percussion and Conversion." (The Gun Report, May 2000)
22. *Civil War Pistols of the Union.* (Lincoln, Rhode Island: Andrew Mowbray Inc. Publishers, 1992) pg. 154 & 157
23. *Civil War Small Arms of the U.S. Navy and Marine Corps.* (Lincoln, Rhode Island: Andrew Mowbray Inc. Publishers, 1999) pg. 128-129

Chapter Six

1. *Civil War Pistols of the Union,* (Lincoln, Rhode Island: Andrew Mowbray Inc./Publishers, 1992) pg. 154.
2. *Arms for Virginia On the Eve of the Civil War: The Armory Commission Letters of Col. Francis H. Smith.* Transcribed & Annotated by Col. Edwin L. Dooley, Jr. Virginia Military Institute, accessed January 2, 2010, http://www.vmi.edu/uploadedFiles/Archives/Records/Correspondence/Francis_Smith/Smith_ArmoryCommissionLetters.pdf. The letters included in this work are the property of the Virginia Military Institute.
3. *Colonel Burton's Spiller & Burr Revolver.* (Macon, Georgia: Mercer University Press, 1996) pg. 24
4. Information provided by Mr. Tim Prince, College Hill Arsenal. www.collegehillarsenal.com

Chapter Seven

1. *Colonel Burton's Spiller & Burr Revolver.* (Macon, Georgia: Mercer University Press, 1996) pg. 7-10
2. *Colonel Burton's Spiller & Burr Revolver.* (Macon, Georgia: Mercer University Press, 1996) pg. 14-15
3. *Colonel Burton's Spiller & Burr Revolver.* (Macon, Georgia: Mercer University Press, 1996) pg. 24
4. *Colonel Burton's Spiller & Burr Revolver.* (Macon, Georgia: Mercer University Press, 1996) pg. 35
5. *Colonel Burton's Spiller & Burr Revolver.* (Macon, Georgia: Mercer University Press, 1996) pg. 45-46
6. *Colonel Burton's Spiller & Burr Revolver.* (Macon, Georgia: Mercer University Press, 1996) pg. 49
7. *Confederate Longarms and Pistols.* (Charlotte, North Carolina: Richard Taylor Hill & William Edward Anthony, Publishers, 1978) pg. 271.
8. *Flayderman's Guide to Antique American Firearms and Their Values.* (Iola, Wisconsin: Gun Digest Books, 2007) pg. 641
9. *American Percussion Revolvers.* (Ottawa, Ontario: Museum Restoration Service, 1971) pg. 158
10. *Flayderman's Guide to Antique American Firearms and Their Values.* (Iola, Wisconsin: Gun Digest Books, 2007) pg. 361
11. *Flayderman's Guide to Antique American Firearms and Their Values.* (Iola, Wisconsin: Gun Digest Books, 2007) pg. 358-359

Chapter Eight

1. *The Whitney Navy Revolver.* (The Gun Report, October 1992) pg. 36
2. *The Whitney Firearms.* (Huntington, West Virginia: Standard Publications, Inc., 1946) pg. 320-328
3. *Remington Army And Navy Revolvers 1861-1888.* (Albuquerque, New Mexico: University of New Mexico Press, 2007) pg. 279-281
4. *A Study of Colt Conversions and Other Percussion Revolvers.* (Iola, Wisconsin: Krause Publications, 1997) pg. 428-430
5. *A Study of Colt Conversions and Other Percussion Revolvers.* (Iola, Wisconsin: Krause Publications, 1997) pg. 430-431

Chapter Nine

1. *Flayderman's Guide to Antique American Firearms and Their Values.* (Iola, Wisconsin: Gun Digest Books, 2007) pg. 276
2. *Civil War Guns.* (Secaucus, New Jersey: Castle, 1982) pg. 288

BIBLIOGRAPHY

Ackerman, Slim. "Frontiersman's Revolver is Found in England." *Muzzle Blasts*, June 1982.

Domina, Ken and Don Ware. *Whitney Navy Revolvers*. Chapter 4, Unpublished Manuscript.

Edwards, William B. *Civil War Guns*. (Secaucus, New Jersey: Castle, 1982)

Flayderman, Norm. *Flayderman's Guide to Antique American Firearms and Their Values*. (Iola, Wisconsin: Gun Digest Books, 2007)

Fuller, Claud E. *The Whitney Firearms*. (Huntington, West Virginia: Standard Publications, Inc., 1946).

Hill, Richard Taylor and William Edward Anthony. *Confederate Longarms and Pistols*. (Charlotte, North Carolina: Self-published, 1978)

Jordan, Robert M. and Darrow M. Watt. *Colt's Pocket '49: It's* [sic] *Evolution including the Baby Dragoon & Wells Fargo*. (Loma Mar, California: Darrow M. Watt, 2000)

Kopec, John, Ron Graham and C. Kenneth Moore. *A Study of the Colt Single Action Army Revolver.* (Printed and bound in South Korea: Graphic Publishers, revised fifth printing 2006)

McAulay, John D. *Civil War Pistols of the Union*. (Lincoln, Rhode Island: Andrew Mowbray Inc. Publishers, 1992)

McDowell, R. Bruce. *A Study of Colt Conversions and Other Percussion Revolvers*. (Iola, Wisconsin: Krause Publications, 1997)

McKee, W. Reid and M.E. Mason, Jr. *Civil War Projectiles II Small Arms & Field Artillery. (*Orange, Virginia: Moss Publications, 1980)

Mowbray, Stuart C. *Civil War Arms Purchases and Deliveries*. (Lincoln, Rhode Island: Andrew Mowbray Inc. Publishers, 2000)

Norman, Matthew W. *Colonel Burton's Spiller & Burr Revolver*. (Macon, Georgia: Mercer University Press, 1996)

Pachanian, Sam and L. Frank Richey. "Marking Variations of U.S. Naval Inspectors on Colt 1851 and 1861 Navy Model Revolvers Percussion and Conversion." (*The Gun Report*, May 2000)

Schreier, Jr., Konrad F. *The Whitney Navy Revolver*. (The Gun Report, October 1992)

Sellers, Frank M. and Samuel E. Smith. *American Percussion Revolvers*. (Ottawa, Ontario: Museum Restoration Service, 1971).

The Eli Whitney Museum and Workshop. "Eli Whitney: The Family." Accessed August 6, 2010. http://www.eliwhitney.org/new/museum/eli-whitney/family

INDEX

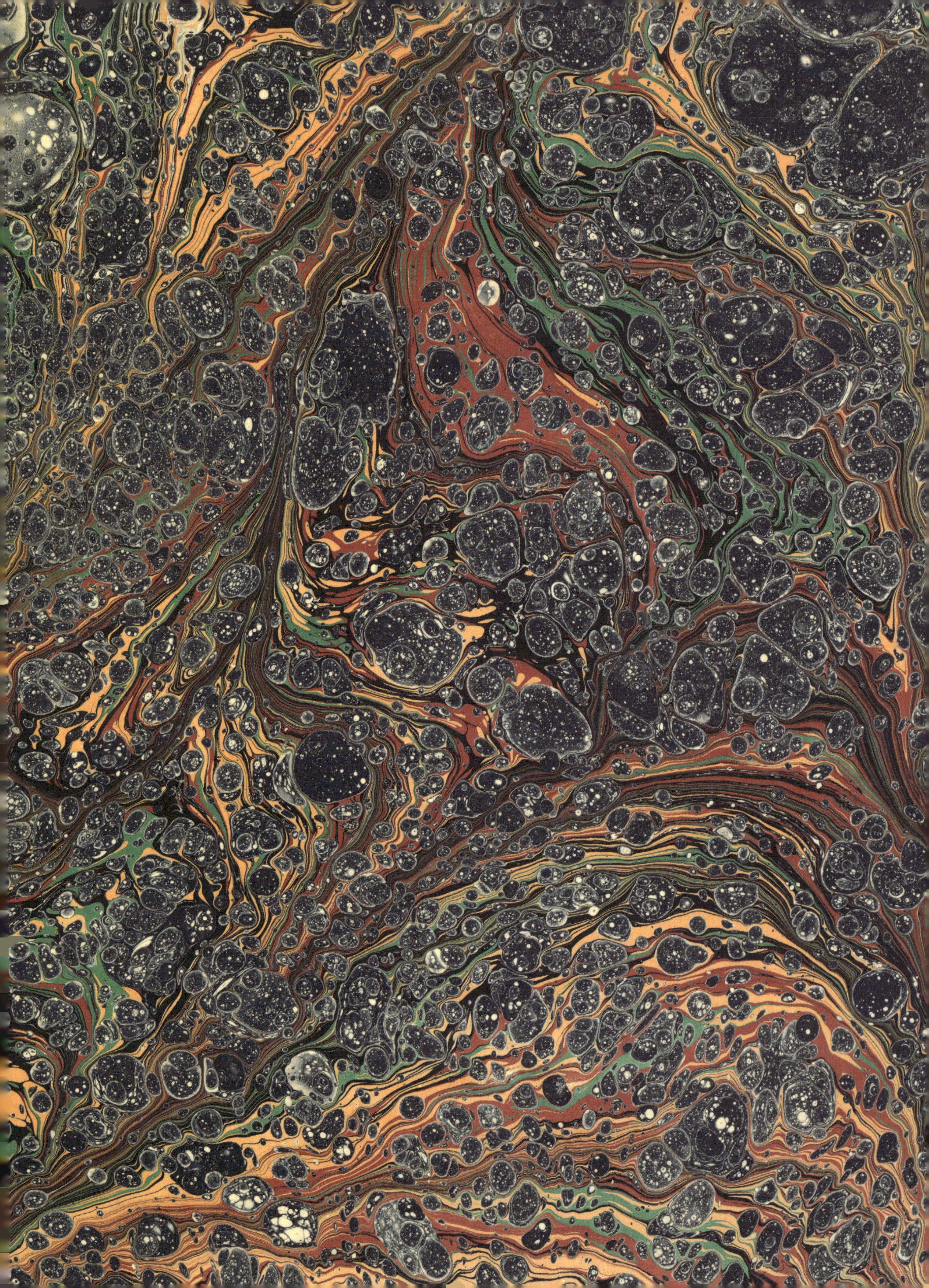